Leading to Excel

Transformation, by definition, is a radical change in outcome – not incremental small movements. Too often organizations claim to have a transformation organization, yet little to no evidence of achieving anything close to the level of significant change from their prior state, let alone compared to its own industry's performance. What are the principles that exist in every transformation?

This book details those principles found across industries including highly competitive automotive global competitors to local healthcare large and small. Leading radical improvement demands leadership "muscle, mentality, and motivation." It demands practice, repetition, and building muscles to "lift" organizations often facing heavy resistance. Those who excel in transformative change achieve a mental state envisioning the future, blocking out disruptions, and help others see the same view of a largely different future. In this book, the author coaches leaders on how to build the muscle, mental state, and motivate oneself and the organization to achieve radical change and focuses on radical improvement against industry competitors. Detailed examples in healthcare, manufacturing, aviation, automotive, and financial services are included to help those who struggle to achieve changes. The author shares his experiences in each of these industries as leaders learned and applied the principles of leading transformations. The author shares screen navigation in Minitab on how to measure, do measurement system analyses, and create in real time. Examples of dashboards and visual management techniques are also included.

Leading to Excel

Principles of Transformation

Richard Morrow

Routledge
Taylor & Francis Group
A PRODUCTIVITY PRESS BOOK

Designed cover image: Shutterstock

First published 2025
by Routledge
605 Third Avenue, New York, NY 10158

and by Routledge
4 Park Square, Milton Park, Abingdon, Oxon, OX14 4RN

Routledge is an imprint of the Taylor & Francis Group, an informa business

Library of Congress Cataloging in Publication Data
Names: Morrow, Richard author
Title: Leading to excel: principles of transformation / Richard Morrow.
Description: New York: Routledge, 2025. | Includes bibliographical references and index. |
Identifiers: LCCN 2025005128 (print) | LCCN 2025005129 (ebook) | ISBN 9781032639567 hardback | ISBN 9781032639550 paperback | ISBN 9781032639574 ebook
Subjects: LCSH: Leadership | Organizational change
Classification: LCC HD57.7 .M6747 2025 (print) | LCC HD57.7 (ebook) | DDC 658.4/092--dc23/eng/20250616
LC record available at https://lccn.loc.gov/2025005128
LC ebook record available at https://lccn.loc.gov/2025005129

ISBN: 9781032639567 (hbk)
ISBN: 9781032639550 (pbk)
ISBN: 9781032639574 (ebk)

DOI: 10.4324/9781032639574

Typeset in Garamond
by Deanta Global Publishing Services, Chennai, India

Dedication

To Janet, my wife who lived these stories with me and for me.

Contents

Preface

Leading to Excel shares stories from some of the largest industries. I researched organizations that achieved significantly large improvements and transformative change to understand if there are principles common regardless of organization, industry, and location.

I will define excellence and transformations in Chapter 1 so readers can calibrate to appreciate how much the organizations shared in this book changed relative to their original performance. Starting with the first transformation story in Chapter 2 of achieving excellence, you may compare your organization and take away the methods and principles valuable in your journey to improve.

Achieving transformative improvements is achieved using eight common principles. It does not matter if you are a leader or stakeholder in a small business, civic group, or the CEO in one of the world's largest publicly held organizations or government.

Sharing successes as well as missteps along the way is important in learning how to improve and achieve goals with speed. Success is more likely by eliminating or mitigating risks to your success. Many of my teammates in these stories have shared their stories honestly and humbly so you, my customer of this book, can benefit.

I have tried to bias content to what you must do well rather than focus on the failures. The missteps I share present the most likely risk and are the most severe. These mistakes or omissions are important to avoid. Some organizations, especially in industries less mature in risk management, may underestimate the risks to achieving goals. Risk management is one of the eight principles and can make or break a transformation. Effective risk management will minimize wasting time when you don't see the risks and failure occurs. I also want you to gain confidence that you can lead an organization to excel and achieve an uncontestable transformation and not scare you so much that you don't try.

Foundationally, I hope you join me in agreeing there is much more to leading an organization to excellence than using the eight principles I find in every transformation. Tom Peters, author of *In Search of Excellence*, noted 50 years ago that leaders who had respect for people and treated them well have led organizations to excellence. Tom shares the transformative change these companies have achieved excellence. Walt Disney and a car dealer in Texas are examples who had achieved excellence in Tom's and his co-author's research, Robert Waterman. Both organizations exist today. My experience is treating team members with humanity whether employees, volunteers, suppliers, customers, or anyone engaged is the foundation of leading to excellence and sustaining it. Put another way, a leader can push and threaten team members to "make the numbers" and maybe even radically improve to a goal, but the outcome will not meet my definition of transformation due to a high probability of not sustaining it.

I hope you enjoy these stories of transformations and find that these eight principles, coupled with treating your team well, result in achieving excellence.

Acknowledgments

Few have been given the opportunities I have enjoyed and toiled in my careers across industries and in life. This book, with its stories of transforming performance and organizations, is my humble gift forward to those who will lead their organizations to excel.

Acknowledgments are an important feature and thank you for reading because readers can get context for what we cover, and this feature is a way to understand potential bias. I start the book with context and address bias, especially when judging excellence. I tell the transformation stories acknowledging those who led organizations to excel, so I use this acknowledgment feature as bookends to the stories you will read in the chapters.

The Opening Bookend

I owe my beginning to my Dad and Mom, to whom I owe my life and my first career aspiration of musical performance. Mom taught me music and dad taught me business. Both complement each other very well. Both music and business taught me the art and science of achieving some really fun goals. Whether seeing great healthcare organizations become greater or performing to hundreds of fans, hard work and following some principles always led to success. Life took me living through business careers to get here - enjoying my first career plan as a musician and continuing to share back via books like this. I cannot come close to naming all I learned and experienced with my parents and my siblings, Mark, and Mike, but I think focusing on faith in God, family, and having the confidence that hard work pays off is learning 101.

My Granddad also gave me my first paying job, driving him on a rural Illinois mail route in our small county where Abraham Lincoln practiced law.

At 16 years of age, what better job is there than driving? We drove mail from the post office to the small rural post offices twice a day. The hours were a bit brutal, starting around 4:30 AM even in the cold, snowy dead of winter, and then again around 3:30 PM for the second run of mail, but the best benefit was being with Granddad.

While in high school we had a band playing what today is called Classic Rock. Of course it took years to call it Classic. Our claim to fame was performing in the same venue that REO Speedwagon, Styx, Cheap Trick, Head East, and other top artists performed but I thought learning music in college would help my career. So off to Eastern Illinois University I went to be a music major but decided on a physics major for a love of science and thinking a rock musician performing is better learning than music theory and all the formal courses as a music major.

During my first year, in college high school friends invited me to perform in their band back in my hometown, two hours from EIU. By the end of my summer break, we were performing at some great outdoor festivals and I decided to transfer to Illinois State University so I could stay in the band, live at home to rehearse and perform, and see where music took me. I even changed my major from science to business because business required the least amount of hours at school, taking me away from performing. Wow – I could get a degree and have no science labs at night, and Business classes could be on just Tuesday and Thursday. Music and Business – they go well together.

Skip ahead after earning a degree and starting a new band, I saw my first love at a party after we performed. Jan Short and I never dated during high school, but we had a blast in high school as friends. I loved her then and now, and I owe being in a band as the catalyst for a life together. After one gig at the afterparty party, I found out she had broken up with her long time boyfriend. Thanks to my Dad and Uncle having taught me how to paint cars, I offered to paint her car and that was enough to shift us from dear friends to getting married. I had almost all I wanted – a wife, degree, a band, and our first home. Buying a house in 1980 with double digit interest rates was a first hurdle, but we bought an 800 square foot one bedroom old house which we renovated ourselves with some family labor for a perfect first home. Life was perfect – except we wanted a family. Faith and Family, remember?

I loved music but I also liked building the band as a business. I learned how to run a business with the band, which paid dividends, so to speak, for life. With my high school friend and younger brother, we started Pulsar and it became one of the most popular bands in Central Illinois, voted the best band, and won Miller Beer's Rock to Riches contest for the area. As my brother Mike, the guitarist, shared recently, it was marketing and promotion that helped Pulsar become one of the largest drawing local bands – not just music. We also learned about the eight principles I find in every transformation as I studied the music industry. I am the first to admit Pulsar did not transform anything but learning how to run a business would aid me in every transformation henceforth.

Jan and I decided our new career was family, and like in so many songs, one or the other had to give. I will never regret my first "retirement" from music to raise a family and enjoy boarding really nice airplanes instead of our band's bus and seeing the world on an expense report at great companies.

The Closing Bookend

The kids have their own families, and we get to be grandparents, which is like being an interim executive. We can come in, rile them up, and then leave when we want. My plan all along was to return to musical performance, and in preparation built a music studio. I retired from the corporate world and am again performing music and enjoying every minute while continuing to author books.

But only a fool ignores the past and refuses to help others with their stories to come. Hard work hasn't stopped and the saying, "I never thought I would value roadies more than groupies" is so true. The band is doing well, but hauling a show around keeps me fit. I haven't retired from the consulting world – just working pro bono. As I was writing this morning, I helped a former colleague mentioned in this book with his next career move. I am kept busy building the band business, having this morning booking our fourth performance at one of our favorite music venues.

Faith, family, and I still have the confidence I can contribute. So, reach out to me if there is anything I can contribute to your journey to excellence – pro bono, of course.

Richard (Rick) Morrow

About the Author

Richard "Rick" Morrow — Author, Executive, Educator, and Organizational Transformation Leader

Richard "Rick" Morrow is a recognized authority in organizational transformation, high reliability, and performance excellence. With more than 25 years of executive and consulting experience, he has guided companies and institutions across healthcare, aviation, automotive, construction, financial services, and technology through large-scale cultural and operational change.

Morrow is the author of *Leading High-Reliability Organizations in Healthcare, Utilizing the 3Ms in Process Improvement, and Utilizing the 3Ms of Process Improvement in Healthcare*, works that have become touchstones for leaders determined to achieve sustainable excellence. His writing translates the rigorous methods of Lean Six Sigma, reliability engineering, predictive analytics, and leadership into practical tools that leaders and individual contributors can use to transform their organizations into cultures of high performance, reliability, safety, and innovation.

As the architect of Lean Six Sigma and High Reliability programs across industries including Eaton Electrical, Motorola, Belmont University, and Penn Medicine at the University of Pennsylvania, Morrow has educated leaders to think beyond incremental improvement and instead pursue transformation. He also developed the Lean Six Sigma Program for The Joint Commission and helped establish its Center for Transforming Healthcare, where he partnered with world-class organizations—including Mayo Clinic, Johns Hopkins, Cedars-Sinai, and Stanford—to redesign processes that reduce harm and elevate quality.

Morrow's approach to transformation is anchored in the principle that **sustained excellence requires both systems change and leadership style changes**. He equips executives with frameworks to improve performance by engineering-in reliability while reducing variation, waste, and harm, while also cultivating cultures that prioritize accountability, collaboration, and innovation. His 3Ms framework—addressing Measuring outcomes and key variables, **M**anaging to those measures, and **M**aking outcomes easier to achieve and sustain - has been especially influential in shifting organizations from firefighting to long-term resilience.

Beyond healthcare, Morrow has implemented global transformation programs for Fortune 500 companies including United Airlines, Eaton, Motorola, and SKF. As a Motorola Master Black Belt and Lean Enterprise certified leader, he has led initiatives that streamlined operations, improved safety, and drove measurable financial performance.

A sought-after speaker at national forums such as the American Society for Quality (ASQ) and the National Patient Safety Foundation (NPSF), Morrow is known for bridging theory with execution. His message is clear: **organizations can achieve the reliability of aviation and nuclear power if leaders commit to transformation at every level**.

This book, *Leading to Excel: Principles of Transformations* answers the next set of questions beginning with how leaders guide their organizations in achieving radical improvement and how to sustain performance. Richard answers what transformations are and the principles of transformations. The book is filled with proven transformations, how the principles were applied, and the key players found throughout the organizations – not just those with leadership in their titles.

Chapter 1

Defining Excellence and Transformation

Setting Up for Success

Chapter 1's purpose is to share the eight principles leading to excel and how to set up a scoreboard to measure success. Understanding how to measure is the key to build confidence in the journey to excellence and ensuring the goal is met and sustained. Your time is too important to spend reading about companies and organizations in books of leadership excellence only to find zero proof in measures of excellence no longer exist.

The principles to achieve excellence and transformational improvements are:

1. Principle 1: Skilled in problem-solving
2. Principle 2: Utilize Measure, Manage to the Measure, and Make it easier (3Ms)
3. Principle 3: Specific Measurable Attainable, Relevant Timebound (SMART) and radical goals exist
4. Principle 4: Strategize using competitive forces and match organizational structure to strategy
5. Principle 5: Engage and go see firsthand
6. Principle 6: Manage risk
7. Principle 7: Celebrate quick wins
8. Principle 8: Keep utilizing the 3Ms

DOI: 10.4324/9781032639574-1

A principle to never do: Attempt change without considering the principles.

Transformations show evidence of every principle. The sequence can and may differ as leaders learn the principles and opportunities arise.

Measurement is how one claims a transformation has occurred. Measures allow us to describe status and change. *Merriam Webster's* definition is: the dimensions, capacity, or amount of something ascertained by measuring for physical measure and adds "an estimate of what is to be expected (as of a person or situation)." I think both definitions fit well in measuring excellence and transformations.

This chapter stands by itself preparing you for assessing any measure of excellence the company purports to have achieved. The method to assess the measurement's ability is called a measurement system analysis (MSA.) You can use this same way to test in every story in this book of organizations claiming to achieve a transformation. Testing a good measure is simply understanding the two qualities of a good measurement system.

X, formerly known as Twitter, discusses its Key Performance Indicator (KPI), Monetizable Daily Active Usage or Users (mDAU), in its 2021 Annual Report.[1]

X essentially provides the outcome of its Measurement System Analysis (MSA) of its most important measure of outcome, mDAU. I share the details to gain appreciation of the complexity and importance for an organization to clearly define its key performance measure(s).

Compare your organization's detail of its measures and how it is measured (Measurement system), and the litmus test is to get consensus from every employee on the KPI, how it is measured, and what it means to the organization. A transformation should affect a KPI, and having this level of detail and understanding gives confidence that the transformation achieved what is shared.

Key Performance Indicator at X

I share directly from X's Annual Report.

We review a number of metrics, including the key metrics discussed below, to evaluate our business, measure our performance, identify trends affecting our business, formulate business plans, and make strategic decisions.

Monetizable Daily Active Usage or Users (mDAU). We define mDAU as people, organizations, or other accounts who logged in or were otherwise authenticated and accessed Twitter on any given day through twitter.com or Twitter applications that are able to show ads. We believe that mDAU, and its related growth, is the best way to measure our success against our objectives and to show the size of our audience and engagement.

We rely on assumptions and estimates to calculate certain of our key metrics, and real or perceived inaccuracies in such metrics may harm our reputation and negatively affect our business.

We calculate our mDAU using internal company data that has not been independently verified. While these numbers are based on what we believe are reasonable calculations for the applicable period of measurement, there are inherent challenges in measuring mDAU and mDAU engagement. For example, there are a number of false or spam accounts in existence on our platform. We estimate that the average number of false or spam accounts during the fourth quarter of 2020 continued to represent fewer than 5% of our mDAU during the quarter. However, this estimate is based on an internal review of a sample of accounts and we apply significant judgment in making this determination. As such, our estimation of false or spam accounts may not accurately represent the actual number of such accounts, and the actual number of false or spam accounts could be higher than we have currently estimated. We are continually seeking to improve our ability to estimate the total number of spam accounts and eliminate them from the calculation of our mDAU, but we otherwise treat multiple accounts held by a single person or organization as multiple accounts for purposes of calculating our mDAU because we permit people and organizations to have more than one account. Additionally, some accounts used by organizations are used by many people within the organization. As such, the calculations of our mDAU may not accurately reflect the actual number of people or organizations using our platform. We regularly review and may adjust our processes for calculating our internal metrics to improve their accuracy. Our measures of mDAU growth and engagement may differ from estimates published by third parties or from similarly titled metrics of our competitors due to differences in methodology. If advertisers, content or platform partners or investors do not perceive our metrics to be accurate representations of our total accounts or mDAU engagement, or if we discover material inaccuracies in our metrics, our reputation may be harmed and content partners, advertisers and platform partners may be less willing to allocate their budgets or resources to our products and services, which could negatively affect our business and operating results. Further, as our business develops, we may revise or cease reporting metrics if we determine that such metrics are no longer accurate or appropriate measures of our performance. If investors, analysts, or customers do not believe our reported measures, such as mDAU, are sufficient or accurately reflect our business, we may receive negative publicity and our operating results may be adversely impacted.

X/Twitter has experienced a turbulent year since Elon Musk came close to purchasing the company, which has in turn raised concerns about the number of bots on the platform. Nevertheless, user numbers have continued to rise. In the last reported quarter, the number of global monetizable daily active users (mDAU) on X/Twitter amounted to 237.8 million users, up from 229 million mDAU in the previous quarter. Overall, this is an increase in mDAU of over 15% when compared to the same quarter of the previous year.

I named this book to be self-evident in its value to you, yet I want to make sure you and I calibrate to ensure a similar understanding. I have heard entirely different definitions of what a transformation is from leaders in charge of transformations. Some of these leaders have the title that includes the word transformation. Therefore, it is important for us to have a common understanding of what a transformation is. I will only cover those changes that have achieved radical change – not small quick changes as one executive defined transformations.

Leading to Excel means leading to achieving radically large change. Leading to Excel is a verb – not a noun denoting a person in a recognized leadership role.

Transformation is an outcome. It is not an organization. In organizations I have consulted or worked in, there is often an inverse correlation between the amount of change and having an office with the word transformation in its name. I will detail examples where transformation titled organizations achieved nothing close to radical change.

Books have been written on leadership, and many claim transformative events have occurred. Many books include valid transformative changes. Who would argue that a book on Abraham Lincoln, the 16th President of the United States, achieved a transformation resulting in abolishing slavery? I have been a fan of medicine's history, and the transformations in medicine have not only resulted in life over death but have also sustained over time. Penicillin and cancer treatment are examples. The principles I share with you were found by studying organizations and their transformations as well as my experience working in global organizations.

Leading to Excel goes beyond sharing stories about successful transformations by recognizing that some of us learn by exploring failures. Thus, I will share anonymously organizations which claimed great success and leadership only to fail in transforming outcomes. We learn from failure, and my hope is to arm you with warning signs on your journey to achieve goals and how to eliminate or mitigate risks so you achieve your goals.

Therefore, my research includes several failures that questions what some publications deem successful. I have personal experiences where colleagues have claimed excellence achieved only to have seen failure to meet the definition of transformation and excellence.

Transformation Defined

Transformation means that a radical change has occurred. Radical is defined as a change in a measure that is unquestionably at a much different level. How different is different enough? In this chapter, I supply an answer and cover a framework for a measurement system used to assess change in any measure. We need to ensure our measurement is telling the truth to claim radical change – a transformation.

Defining a transformation should include a time element. Is it a transformation simply looking at the change in revenue from 20 years ago and not accounting for inflation's impact on the change? Is a change made in 1 day impossible to be considered non-transformative? No, not necessarily. Truly great improvements can be achieved in a short time, but we need to think of time as another fundamental criterion used to judge truth, which I cover in this chapter. The measure must support true change in outcome and sustained vs. a measure that is not apples-to-apples, such as a change in financial outcomes heavily inflated due to inflation.

Radical Change

We need to define radical because we use the term to differentiate non-transformational change from transformational change. A radical change is a level reached that has never, or seldom ever, been achieved. This definition of radical change works regardless of the direction of change.

The experience level of the system being studied for transformative change is important to understand. If one is measuring something very new such as a new process, any good measurement system will see changes in outcome. Discrimination is a term used in assessing a good measurement system – the system can discriminate changes. When defining a transformation, we want to know if there has been enough time to know if the outcome has reached a new level of performance and sustained it. Simply defining radical as achieving a level of performance seldom or never seen before when a process is just starting is not enough. Any measurement system or process just beginning will have a change from a level of performance that was never experienced before. So, we need to clearly state the time frame when declaring a transformation or radical change occurred. It means a lot more when a team states that the performance in 20 years has never been at this level vs. claiming a new process hit a new level of performance on its second day.

There are Two Types of Research and Data

1. Quantitative
2. Qualitative

Too often, transformations have used qualitative "data" to validate that a transformation occurred. Leaders who want to excel will understand both types of data and utilize them correctly, giving confidence to the organization that transformation has occurred.

We need to understand data types first to appreciate that quantitative data provides benefits over qualitative data when the measurement system is proven reliable.

Quantitative Measurement Systems

Quantitative data allows numerical or counting methods to measure the impact. [See Table 1.1.] Examples include quantitative measures like counts, dimensions, weight, currency, time, and even the frequency of sound and light waves.

- A. Continuous (Variable data). (Any point on a histogram is possible, such as in measured and decimal subdivisions)
  - Variable data can be subdivided into finer increments of precision
    - Time (seconds)
    - Speed (ft/min)
    - Rate (inches/time)
    - Dimensions (millimeters)
- B. Discrete (attribute data)
  - Numerical responses that can be counted where divisions between points are not possible

- Good or bad counts
- Number of people
- Number of errors

Quantitative Data Types (Table 1.1)

Table 1.1 Quantitative Data Types

Measure	*Scale (Ratio Has a True Zero Value, Interval Does Not)*
Length (meters, yards, miles)	Ratio
Age (years, months)	Ratio
Volume (liters, cubic inches)	Ratio
Temperature (degrees)	Interval
Time (hours, minutes)	Ratio

Qualitative Measurement Systems

A measure using judgment without numerical data is a qualitative measure. One senses a change and the degree of change. Think of the many satisfaction surveys we are asked to take. The smiley, neutral, and frown emojis are popular. I enjoyed my bi-weekly trek through London Heathrow Airport about as much as getting a tooth pulled, but I smiled the first day when I saw how London Heathrow (LHR) Customs gathered traveler satisfaction. LHR had a pedestal with the three emoji faces and a button to push based on your judgment of the experience. The placement in the Customer process was important to capture the passenger's opinion after a traveler's luggage is in hand and much of the anxiety is gone. This qualitative and simple measurement system is not what I recommend for judging if a transformation occurred. I will give tips how to improve the way to measure a transformation. Unfortunately, even this measurement system is more valid than some systems used by those who claim transformations.

- Qualitative (Categorical Responses) – variables for which an attribute or classification is measured.

  Yes or No
  Good or Bad
  Meets the standard, does not

Which Is Better?

Quantitative measures usually meet the tests of a good measurement system better because:

- Variation is more discerning
- More options for analysis
- Affects data collection plan
- Allows any response possible
- Requires a smaller sample size than discrete
- Shows trends faster

Example Using Music

To understand data types, let's use an example of data that most would consider qualitative – music. Music is a creative way to define radical. Music is very often measured qualitatively, such as naming a favorite song or artist, and critics abound judging the quality of a performance. Yet music theory has mathematical measures, such as the measure of the frequency in sound waves, which can explain the pleasantness of sound or describe dissonance.

I am in a music group and my personal goal has been to improve the range of my voice. Stated musically, I want to be able to sing higher frequency notes that happen to be higher than the G note above Middle C. Musical notes are measured using hertz, abbreviated Hz. The A above Middle C is at 440 Hz. If my highest note is E which is lower than A 440, then a radical change for me measured in frequency is being able to sing at 440 Hz from my current ability at E which is 349 Hz. This change equals a 91 Hz increase in range. Believe me, that is a radical improvement for me.

Another way to determine a radical change is through the use of statistical process control (SPC). I cover examples and much more on what SPC is and why it is the hallmark method for judging if a transformation occurs. I cover SPC with examples and how to easily apply SPC in a later chapter. For now, think of SPC as a way to assess the probability of a transformation. If it is highly improbable a measure would ever be reached as seen in the SPC chart method, and now the team is reaching that level routinely, then a radical change – a transformation has occurred.

Measurement System Analysis for Transformation

A measurement system is required to make a measurement. A measurement system is composed of everything necessary to measure. A measurement system used in cutting a piece of paper to a specific length might be an instruction on using a pair of scissors, a person, and a ruler or tape measure. Missing any of these components results in an inability to measure. Measuring a transformation is more complex than cutting paper, and a measurement system often has a process instruction on how to measure.

Leaders must have a capable measurement system of performance, and readers want the confidence that stories of excellence and achieving transformations are true. The easiest definition of a good measurement system is one that results in truth. The measurement system, the way one measures, must be understood, and the result must be believed. We benefit from using the statistical method of defining a good measurement system. A good measurement system will be **repeatable and reproducible** regardless who measures or which components are used in the measurement system.

An example of repeatability is in weighing ourselves. In the morning before a doctor's office visit, I weigh myself using my bathroom scale. If each time I step on the scale I get the same weight, the same weight repeats each time I step on the scale, this is good repeatability.

For reproducibility, think of what happens when the nurse weighs you at the doctor's office. I am not sure about you, but the nurse's process never results in the same weight as when I weighed myself at home less than 30 minutes earlier. The measurement system is not reproducing the same weight. This is poor reproducibility.

Using Twitter's Annual Report, Twitter highlights the potential harm of poor reproducibility. Its Annual Report states: *Our measures of mDAU growth and engagement may differ from estimates published by third parties or from similarly titled metrics of our competitors due to differences in methodology. If advertisers, content or platform partners or investors do not perceive our metrics to be accurate representations of our total accounts or mDAU engagement, or if we discover material inaccuracies in our metrics, our reputation may be harmed and content partners, advertisers and platform partners may be less willing to allocate their budgets or resources to our products and services, which could negatively affect our business and operating results.*

Consulting companies have latched onto the transformation word promoting their consulting services have helped clients achieve transformations. The consulting firms claiming such should have a measurement system that results in a judgment that clients achieved radical improvement (Seldom, if ever, do I see bragging about a client that achieved a transformational failure).

To assess the firm's ability to help clients transform performance, simply apply the two tests, repeatability and reproducibility, to their claims of transformation. If the consultants on the contract all agree the client achieved a transformation, that is meeting the repeatability test of a good measurement system – aka claim. Now, ask the client the same question. If the client agrees it achieved a transformation, that is meeting the test of reproducibility. A failure in repeatability and/or reproducibility suggests considering the success suspect. Either the measurement system is flawed, or a transformation may not have occurred.

This is not to say that 100% of every employee, especially in large organizations, will agree on all aspects in the qualitative judgment of excellence when quantitative analysis is not available. The arduousness an individual applies and political motives play into so many judgments. The political parties in the United States provide too many examples of completely polar conclusions in "measuring" the same event. Readers simply need to have confidence in their ability to do a Measurement System Analysis.

I applied these tests before using the stories of excellence and transformation. All contributors were under the same measurement system that I used on my personal experiences. Too often, books claiming the secret to leading fail the test of reproducibility when the organization that was promoted as excellent fails and no longer exists, even under another name. At printing, the organizations I share of successful transformations from my career are still operating, although some have grown and been renamed.

Some leaders may be trying to improve employee satisfaction. There are many ways to measure satisfaction, and a common measurement system is the rate of attrition. Too many employees voluntarily leaving the organization may be a sign of dissatisfaction. The measurement includes having to define, "too many." If the leader's judgment is that the attrition rate is acceptable and the Human Resources department believes the attrition rate is a sign of dissatisfaction, the measurement system is not reproducible.

Work needs to be done so that the measurement system results in truth for these stakeholders. Understanding the measurement system well may also provide hints on what to improve. Note that I purposely did not include employee judgment. Hmmm, maybe if the employees were involved in the measurement system, truth might be gained?

Obviously, a transformation requires a measurement system, even if it is judgmental. One must strive for a measure that is believed to have little chance of bias.

Quantitative data allow tests of repeatability and reproducibility to be performed more easily, and one may see progress earlier, allowing what we call Principle 6 – Celebrating quick wins to kick in and accelerate improvement. We will cover all the principles and relate back to measuring excellence and transformations through every story of transformation.

Mixing Quantitative and Qualitative Measurement

We have already mixed data types. We discussed quantitatively measuring change, but labeling the change "radical" is a judgment – qualitative. What we did, though, is consider a quantitative measure to define radical – a change in Hz higher than I ever sang before.

Transformations may be measured qualitatively, and often only qualitatively, which is common. The point of this book is to understand and know how to lead organizations to excel to a level of transformative change with confidence and a good measurement system is fundamental for buy-in. Don't let having only qualitative measurements hinder your journey.

I advise always trying to measure anything quantitatively because of the qualities of repeatability and reproducibility that are higher with quantitative measurement systems than qualitative but sometimes all we have are qualitative measures. Examples include judgment, feel, look, happiness, and pain.

This brings us to a qualitative aspect of even quantitatively measured changes. A qualitative measure is not one that can be counted – it is often a judgment. So, who is to judge how much of a change is radical? Using risk management concepts, maybe the answer lies in the cost of being wrong – the cost of disagreement. I leave it to each organization to assess, but I offer my judgment rules:

Let's start with pain. Healthcare has tried to take the qualitative measure of pain one is having and make it quantitative. A caregiver may decide to give pain management (a pain reducer medication) based on a patient's response using a scale of one to ten. A doctor may ask a patient complaining of pain to give a number for the pain. The doctor, nurse, or therapist will help the patient calibrate the patient's measure by stating rate the pain as a ten if the pain is unbearable – the worst pain the patient has experienced.

To discriminate changes in pain over time, the caregiver helps the patient use a scale from 0 to 10 and may describe a pain level of 5 as painful but not debilitating, while a level of 0 or 1 indicates very little pain, which the patient may not feel the need to manage. Pain is still qualitative, but having a way to quantify it helps decision-making, and calibration is easier because it is based on the patient's own qualitative judgment.

Figure 1.1 Smiley face.

- 0 = No pain
- 1 = Some pain but do not notice it most of the time.
- 2 = Pain constant but not enough to stop what I am doing.
- 3 = Pain is considerable and I would like it to be reduced significantly.
- 4 = Very bad pain. About the most pain I have had.

The smiley face measurement system used in the airport example is useful again. Some may add numerical values to the smiley/frown emojis but not implying numerical counting.

A Popular Transformation Mixed Measure

Transformations in customer and employee satisfaction have occurred and are almost always useful to learn about because of the common goals many organizations have: happy employees and companies.

I would bet you have been asked to rate a company using a scale of 0–10 on your likelihood to recommend. This question was popularized in a book, "*The Ultimate Question*."[3]

The question typically uses a scale of 0 to 10, where 10 is to be used if a person would definitely recommend the company to a friend or relative and 0 if they would definitely not recommend. The measurement system is truly qualitative, and the numerical scale allows quantitative analysis and reference over time.

The review of "*The Ultimate Question*" book on Amazon itself is interesting.

> This is the review: You also generate a vital metric: your Net Promoter Score (NPS).[3] Since the book was first published, the Net Promoter Score has transformed companies, across industries and sectors, constituting a game-changing system and ethos that rivals Six Sigma in its power.

The book review on Amazon uses the word "transformation" in promoting the book and compares the value of the concept to Six Sigma. Yet no measure of transformation is given as proof companies have been transformed in this review. The authors share data in the stories, however. The other interesting point in the review is that NPS is an example of a qualitative measure utilizing a quantitative measurement system. Net Promoter Score is a ratio of the percent of those recommending the company minus the percent of those who do not recommend. I have used the NPS and Ultimate Question technique with Six Sigma's powerful methods for years, and this book covers how the NPS measurement system and Six Sigma were successful in transforming the patient experience in healthcare.

I suggest considering a quantitative measurement when working with only a qualitative measurement system. Keep in mind that the numerical measure should not be a complete substitute because there is judgment involved in how well the numerical scale correlates with changes in judgment. Additionally, it may mask the quality of the qualitative measure and, worse, create errors in the measure resulting in wrong conclusions.

Risk Management Begins with Measuring Risk

Principle 6: Manage Risk is another measurement system utilizing a mix of qualitative and quantitative data types and a critical principle in not only achieving excellence but also preventing change from adding risk. This principle exposes how a transformative change may erode and return to the prior state.

Risk management includes measuring risk, and three variables help measure risk. These three are:

1. Severity of the risk
2. Occurrence or probability of the risk
3. Detectability of the risk so the elimination or mitigation of the risk may occur before failure.

Many industries, in fact everyone I have worked with, use a Failure Mode and Effects Analysis (FMEA) method or a similar concept to manage risk identification and prioritization of risk. Table 1.2 is an example of the FMEA form used by teams to identify and then prioritize risks. Often the scoring is a qualitative measure. Some quantitative data may exist and should be used, such as the count of occurrences for the Occurrence variable. Included in this simple FMEA form are definitions of the Severity, Occurrence, and Detectability variables. To assist teams in converting qualitative risks quantitatively, a rating scale is often used. See Table 1.3.

Again, fine-tune the scoring criteria to best fit your design, process, or system requiring risk management.

Failure Mode and Effects Analysis Example

Table 1.2 Failure Mode and Effects Analysis Example

Potential Failure Modes and Effects Analysis (PFMEA)										
Item or Process	*Emergency*		*Process Responsibility*	*Nancy – Director*			*Prepared by:*	*Adam*		
Core team	*Emergency department staff*						*PFMEA Latest Revision Date*		*1/1/2026*	
Process Step or Function	*Input*	*Potential Failure Mode*	*Potential Effect(s) of Failure*	*Severity*	*Potential Cause(s)/ Mechanisms of Failure*	*Occurrence*	*Current Process Controls Prevention*	*Current Process Controls Detection*	*Detection*	*Risk Priority Number (RPN)*
Include step from Process Map in all rows for sorting	*Include input from Process Map in all rows for sorting*	*Failure or symptom evidenced in the output*	*Impact on the customer requirements*	*How Severe is the effect to the customer?*	*Causes to input failure. Add row for each cause within step/ Input*	*How often does cause or FM occur?*	*Existing controls that prevent the cause or the Failure Mode*	*Existing controls that detect the cause or the Failure Mode before defects escape*	*How well can you detect cause or failure mode?*	
Assessment	Emergency department on-call physician	Late to arrive	Anxiety	6	Very high demand (10 times the mean) due to bus accident	2	None	Early responder notice to ED	8	96
Assessment	Emergency department physician	Unable to understand patient	Slow to access	2	Patient inarticulate	5	None	Triage identifies issue	1	10
Patient comes to emergency department	Hospital staff	Congestion	Patient waits	9	Very high demand (10 times the mean) due to bus accident	2	None	Early responder notice to ED	8	144
Patient comes to emergency department	Patient	Patient refuses treatment	Returns after recurring symptoms	9	Concern about cost	4	None	Posted cost support but not very visible	1	36

A Rating Scale and Failure Mode and Effects Analysis Risk Form

Table 1.3 Rating Scale Example for Failure Mode & Effects Analysis

Rating	*Severity of Effect*	*Likelihood of Occurrence*	*Ability to Detect*
10	Hazardous without warning	Very high: Failure is almost inevitable	Can not detect
9	Hazardous with warning		Very remote chance of detection
8	Loss of primary function	High: Repeated failures	Remote chance of detection
7	Reduced primary function performance		Very low chance of detection
6	Loss of secondary function	Moderate: Occasional failures	Low chance of detection
5	Reduced secondary function performance		Moderate chance of detection
4	Minor defect noticed by most customers		Moderately high chance of detection
3	Minor defect noticed by some customers	Low: Relatively few failures	High chance of detection
2	Minor defect noticed by discriminating customers		Very high chance of detection
1	No effect	Remote: Failure is unlikely	Almost certain detection

The team members and experts who know the process well add risks seen in the past and brainstorm all possible risks. Then they use the measurement system to score the risks. Most FMEAs involve qualitative data, and then a quantitative score is assigned. The Risk Priority Number (RPN) at the far right is a quantitative way to prioritize the risks, which are often subjectively scored, to work on.

Principle 5 Engage and Go See is vital to identifying the risks. Risks may be everywhere and learning from those closest to the work or design must occur to gain confidence that the right risks will be managed.

Leaders: Excellence is achieved and sustained with this risk management process. In your efforts to excel, starting with an FMEA often highlights failures that, when eliminated, will lead to improvements. Enough of these risks managed or eliminated may be all one needs to achieve a transformation.

> *Transformation can, and most often, occur from small incremental improvements – if all principles are practiced. Any one principle missing may result in a short term improvement.*

Keeping Score Leading to Excel

Keeping score is key. Four of the eight principles are based on keeping score.

Principle 2: 3 Ms – Measure, Manage to the Measure, and Make it easier

Principle 6: Manage Risk – Risk management includes measuring occurrence probability, severity, and detecting risks, and then how the risk is reduced

Principle 7: Celebrate quick wins. Who doesn't cheer when the favored ball team scores?

Principle 8: Keep Utilizing the 3Ms

Principles 2 and 8 are critical in achieving excellence. How would one know excellence is achieved if there is no measure; the first of three Ms? Measuring without managing to the measure is worse than not measuring. Measuring takes energy and resources, so one should only measure what one wants to manage. Regardless of whether one can control the outcome, leaders who excel measure the input variables, those variables that drive the outcomes, and manage those input variables. Transformations in this book are only achieved by a measure. There are no transformations mentioned without the measure. Now that you know the importance of measuring progress during the journey to excellence, let's develop the scoreboard so all can see. An example of one transformation is in Figure 1.2.

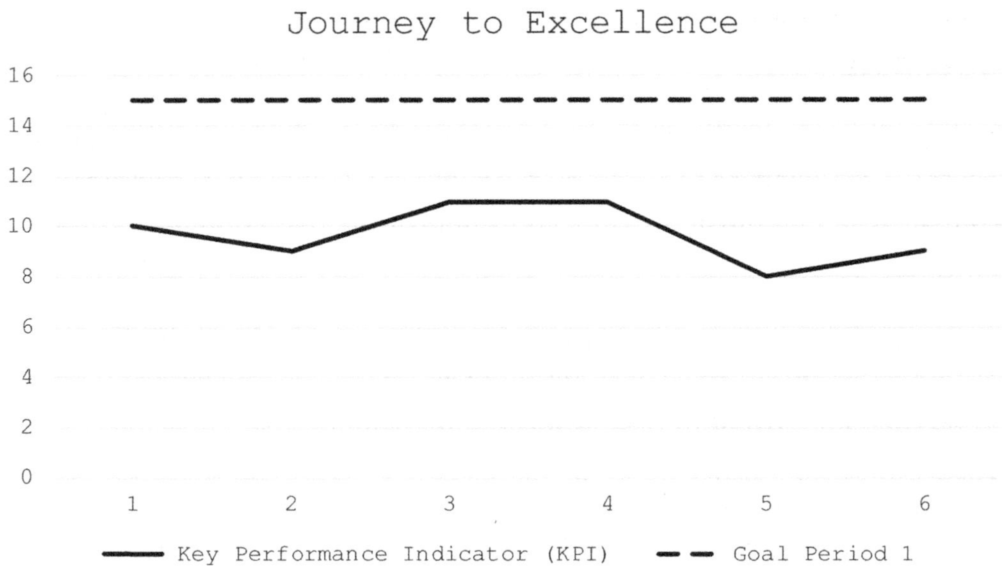

Figure 1.2 Problem solving tool.

Our KPI is, by definition, the measure that defines excellence. A KPI is the outcome measure that will determine if a transformation has been achieved.

A scoreboard will have the KPI, points scored in a game, prominently displayed, illustrating the measure's importance.

KPIs are outcomes, and the rule in performance improvement is to find the input variables that correlate with changes in the outcome. Innings pitched may be a Key Input Variable (KIV) in a baseball game if one believes pitchers become less effective after a number of pitches have occurred.

Scoreboards, therefore, should include not only the key outcome KPIs but also KIVs. Team members should monitor changes in the KIVs and, with skills in correlation, be able to predict changes in the KPIs.

The updated chart now shows a KIV. See Figure 1.3.

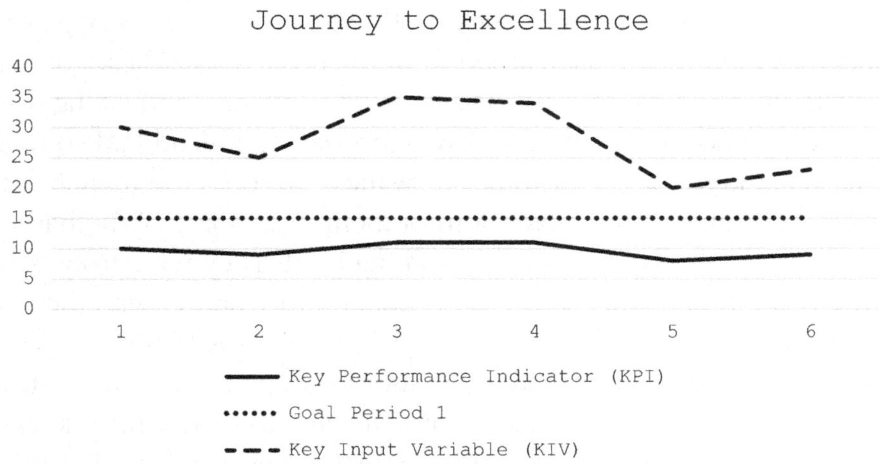

Figure 1.3 Journey to Excellence.

Note how the KPI tracks with the KIV. If the KPI goes up when the KIV goes up, we call this a positive correlation. An example is the number of hits. The more hits a team gets, the higher the score.

KIVs may also be negatively correlated, and negatively correlated variables are just as valuable in predicting changes in the KPI. Going back to innings pitched by the pitcher, the higher the count of innings pitched, the lower the probability of a team's win vs. loss ratio.

When to Post the Score

Now! Post it now. And continue in real time! Utilizing the 3Ms is best achieved by applying the measure as soon as the outcome is measurable. Imagine a baseball or rugby game if the scoreboard only changes the score the day after the game. Look at your organization's scoreboard and KPIs. Do you see the score as soon as the outcome changes? Why not? What value is there in waiting?

Seriously, I see delays in sharing key measures with staff almost everywhere I work, almost everywhere I consult, and I have seen it at my kids' ball games when they only change the score after the end of an inning or a period. Drives you nuts, too?

Do you think great sports teams adjust their game based on the score? Do successful coaches coach without looking at the score? Maybe you think the score is so bad that you are protecting your team from reality by only posting it later than the action?

I share the story of Marc and Chuck. Both were frontline supervisors in one of the factories I led. I had just learned from my boss' boss at headquarters that we were late on shipping products and backorders were months long. I was shocked and had no idea the factory I was just named to lead had so many shipments late and so late to customers. I walked out onto the manufacturing floor where Marc and Chuck were. Both of them were some of the hardest working supervisors and were always working hard. They were truly two of the best in the plant, both getting production out and in working with the team.

I asked, "Marc, Chuck, did you know we are months behind in backlog?" They both answered no and were even more shocked than I was. How can two of the most important management team members not have known about the number one measure of this factory? I went back to the office and found that no one ever provided to them the KPI. However, Marc and Chuck did know about a couple of KIVs with one being the amount of output per hour spent. You might say that makes sense. After all, getting products made has to be a key outcome of any manufacturing plant. And the answer is yes, unless the products made are not the products customers want.

Marc and Chuck were told what products to make based on a forecast of the best guess of what customers might want. Leadership had for a long time thought frontline supervisors didn't need to know what customers ordered, and even if they did, it would be cruel because leadership sent parts for only products leadership thought they should build.

Marc, Chuck, and I rethought this old practice and decided to let every frontline employee know the truth about the huge backorder. We fretted a bit about whether employees would collapse under the news. Instead, we felt that our teammates would appreciate knowing the bad news and rise to the challenge to eliminate the backorder.

We did tell them, and they did step up to the challenge. It was one of the first transformations among many that this team achieved in a short few years. I am still so proud of Marc, Chuck, and the hundreds of frontline employees on the team. Transformations are more than just radically moving the needle – they are a great human story.

Al Houser, the Controller of the larger plant, was a major leader in the overall transformation of the facility, and we will detail his many contributions in a later chapter. I give him credit for getting us the customer backlog first thing in the morning – and every morning. The scoreboard was initially a computer printout that was simply shared with the factory every morning. Everyone could see the scoreboard, and this is Principle 2: Utilizing the 3Ms; Measure what is important, Manage to the measure, and Make it easier to win. The scoreboard itself made all three Ms happen for all.

Where to Post the Scoreboard

Post the scoreboard everywhere your team is. That simple.

Now you know how to create truthful statuses of measures to know where you are on the journey to excellence and transformative change. You know to put the score up for all to see. Let's now learn the eight principles I found in every transformation in every industry.

Principles Leading to Excel

I find these principles in every transformation. Following them is a must not only to achieve excellence but also to sustain it. An organization can start with any of the first six principles and become proficient in any of the eight at different rates. This flexibility makes getting started on the journey easier. Seeing progress in just one principle may be the catalyst that enables the organization to achieve a transformation in outcomes, making the principles themselves the motivator toward a transformation.

Transformations show evidence of every principle. The sequence can and may differ as leaders learn the principles and opportunities arise. Sometimes we hit a roadblock in progressing in a principle, so look at the other seven principles and get to work.

In the example with Marc and Chuck, we didn't start getting the order backlog the next day, but that didn't stop Marc and Chuck from getting teams started on problem-solving. They knew the processes well enough to focus on some of the products with the worst backlog and find the root causes.

Principle 1: Develop Problem-Solving Skills

Marc and Chuck were great leaders of problem-solving and engaged employees in the processes to eliminate the root cause. Oh, I just mentioned Principle 5: Engage = Go See. Marc and Chuck didn't have to go see because they lived on the floor in the processes, so maybe they had an advantage over those organizations that separated management into nice, air-conditioned offices, whereas Marc and Chuck had their desks out on the production floor.

The end of their story together tells a tale of a true transformation. Marc and Chuck retired after many years at the same factory. Even though the products changed, every product line Marc and Chuck led achieved high on-time performance after their first transformation. They practiced the principles and led each of their teams over the years to excellence.

Summary

Excellence is achieved by following principles that include a scoreboard keeping track of success along the journey. Every transformation I experienced and every story I researched includes these same principles.

To improve the probability of achieving excellence, start by ensuring the organization can measure success. The measure of improvement and transformational change begins with ensuring your measurement system is assessing truthfully. The two qualities of a good method to measure are the ability to repeat and to reproduce the measure.

Measuring quantitatively, numerically, is preferred because tests of repeatability and reproducibility are often easier than more subjective, qualitative measures, such as a person's judgment without any numerical data to support the judgment.

Even if qualitative measures are the only option, using numerical ratings that are repeatable and reproducible may build confidence where an organization is in its progress.

Use the FMEA to identify why you aren't where you want to be in performance and throughout your journey to excellence and beyond to sustain. If you don't sustain, it's not a transformation.

Relax about the order of principles deployed. The eight principles do not have to be practiced in order, and any one of them is a great start leading to excel.

Notes

1. Found at https://www.annualreports.com/HostedData/AnnualReports/PDF/NYSE_TWTR_2021.pdf
2. Sources: Hicks, CL., von Baeyer, CL., Spafford, P., van Korlaar, I., and Goodenough, B. The Faces Pain Scale – Revised: Toward a common metric in pediatric pain measurement. *Pain* 2001;93:173–183; Bieri, D., Reeve, R., Champion, GD., Addicoat, L., and Ziegler, J. The Faces Pain Scale for the self-assessment of the severity of pain experienced by children: Development, initial validation and preliminary investigation for ratio scale properties. *Pain* 1990;41:139–150.
3. Reicheld, Fred, and Markey, Rob. *The Ultimate Question 2.0 (Revised and Expanded Edition): How Net Promoter Companies Thrive in a Customer-Driven World,* Harvard Business review Press, September 20, 2011.

Chapter 2

A Comprehensive Transformation

Product, Organizational Structure, Supply Chain, and Information

Let us get started with a transformation. The eight principles will be shared as they occurred. I will share what went well and what did not and include eyewitness accounts including those who led the organization to excel. This first transformation story includes not only transforming one Key Performance Indicator (KPI), but this organization also itself was transformed, and the customer and supply chain. Thus, we get a picture of multiple transformations in one story and it has a happy ending. Most of the radical improvements are still in place 45 years and more later. I also give credit to those who came after this story for sustaining and improving upon the excellence achieved back in the late 1980s and 1990s. Our and their story begins.

Background

Industry: Manufacturing/Distribution
Where: Eaton Corporation Lincoln Plant. Lincoln, IL
Organization: Manufacturing and distribution facility
Markets served by this facility: The Americas primarily

Products/Services: Electrical Power Distribution products. Residential/Commercial/Industrial circuit breakers, loadcenters, and metering enclosures.

DOI: 10.4324/9781032639574-2

This facility was also the largest distribution center for products made in Lincoln giving it a unique capability in getting products to customers quickly. In the mid-1990s, the distribution center slowly converted to manufacturing space with distribution moved to regional centers

History of the Facility

Eaton Corporation purchased Cutler-Hammer in 1978. Competitors included Square-D (Groupe Schneider), General Electric, Westinghouse, Siemens, and others. In case you are wondering how many of the transformations we will discuss have faded away as flash in the pans, the Lincoln Plant continues today still manufacturing many of the same loadcenters and metering devices.

This story is a comprehensive transformation affecting many facets of an organization. I lead with this one because it gives context to the scope some organizations achieve and comparison for readers attempting to radically improve more than a product or service. A transformation of the organization, financial management, and information/reporting makes this story inclusive of the most popular reasons significant improvement is strategically needed. First, we will cover the key players but important to note that every level of the business was involved including the frontline employees, the firm's suppliers, and even customers. I cover some of the leaders' backgrounds in this story to understand they came up through the ranks. The CEO was a financial analyst in his first role at Eaton and the three middle managers, me included, began our careers at entry level positions. My first job was on the frontline in manufacturing in the summer between university semesters.

Leaders Key in the Transformation

Eaton is a global $20.9 billion diversified industrial manufacturer.

Corporate CEO – Alexander M. Cutler (Sandy as he humbly preferred) was our General Manager at Eaton Corporation leading the Industrial Power and Control Distribution Operations at the beginning of this transformation story. He was promoted to President of the Industrial Group during the transformation. Sandy created an environment promoting transformation across the division.

In May 2016[1] Sandy became Chairman and CEO of Eaton Corporation. He spent 41 years moving up from 1980 as a financial analyst, plant manager, controller, and operations executive.

He began his career with Cutler-Hammer in 1975 as a financial analyst and became Business Group Controller in 1977. After Eaton acquired Cutler-Hammer, he was made a division controller in 1979, and in 1980, was appointed Plant Manager of the Atlanta Assembly Plant.

Business Unit – Pete Krol, General manager of the business unit. Pete reported to Sandy heading the Residential Products group. Jim Sternweis, Controller, was instrumental in capital decisions supporting the transformation. Don Link was the Development Engineering leader for the residential and industrial circuit breaker products.

Lincoln Plant – Key leaders were Bill Kelly, Plant Manager. Reporting to Bill were Al Houser, plant Controller, Wayne Boatman, Lincoln's Manufacturing Manager, and Jim Campbell who led Quality. Don McCann led Human Resources and was instrumental in many ways including the significant culture shift required and managing the collective bargaining unit changes required in the transformation. I was in the role of Industrial Engineering Manager and its first Focused Factory Manager.

Special considerations go to the Material Management team, IT, and every single frontline employee and supervisor whose work lives changed whether they helped create the transformation or simply were affected by it. There are countless others who led the transformation from the top leadership to the hourly employees who stepped up in amazing ways.

State before the Transformation

Cost pressures were constant in this highly competitive residential, commercial, and industrial electrical power distribution products business. We were not the market leader and all major competitors had shifted manufacturing offshore chasing lower labor costs. Our customer satisfaction was high and quality was considered in the top two with the market leader. The market leader had much higher volume and market share.

Cutler-Hammer relocated its manufacturing of circuit breakers and enclosures around 1960 from Wisconsin to this small central Illinois town. Its strategy was to lower the cost of manufacturing to compete. Moving plants for lower costs to manufacture seems to be a never-ending practice.

The transformation's purpose may have been to dramatically lower costs, but the Lincoln transformation beginning in the 1980s was much more than just lowering costs. Lincoln needed to transform to remain viable in the increasingly cost-competitive industry. In fact, the transformation effort was to avoid relocating manufacturing. Relocation cost reductions are often short-lived as Cutler-Hammer's attempt to escape collective bargaining in Milwaukee during the 1950s proved only to be unionized soon after transferring to Lincoln.

Principle 4: Strategize Using Competitive Forces

The intensely competitive situation demanded a radical improvement in cost and operations. Through the 1980s the competitive cost pressures kept increasing and Lincoln was falling behind.

Just-In-Time (JIT) manufacturing was becoming popular. Many reported Japanese firms being able to cut the time from suppliers through manufacturing and finally to the customer. The electrical devices that Lincoln made had many permutations and we needed to speed the time from order until delivery to the customer. And we could not afford to stock every permutation. We saw a competitive advantage from speeding products from order entry to customer receipt. This included our supply chain from order to delivery as a competitive advantage, especially because all our competitors increased its supply chain lead time by moving offshore. If we could keep manufacturing in the USA where we sold most of our products, we avoided the supply chain costs everyone who moved offshore incurred.

A Comprehensive Transformation Case Study

I share the prior and current states before the transformation begin to better understand the hundreds of improvements made during the transformation. Many transformations are not a single process change. Many transformations reach back into the design of the product or service to achieve the radical improvements. Lincoln's transformation included design, process, organizational structure, employee pay, supplier design and process, distribution processes, and even customer process changes.

Lincoln, to stay competitive, needed to reduce costs. The design of the residential line of circuit breakers was tackled to reduce its cost by 40% in 3 years. The redesign of the circuit breaker was aptly named "C40/3." This goal was specific, measurable, attainable (we thought), relevant to the strategy, and time bound.

But the circuit breaker was not the only product needing improved competitive costs. All product lines were competing on costs to maintain and grow sales. No process or design was ignored. Lincoln needed a total facility transformation besides the design pressure. Lincoln's goal was to improve productivity and reduce inventory across the facility. The higher costs were labor and inventory. Although inventory carrying expense is a specific measurable goal, the cost of inventory is also the opportunity cost of the space to store inventory that could be used for revenue generating production.

Lincoln's spark was very much the need to compete better. Sandy Cutler, Pete Krol, our marketing leader, and we all saw sales were not gaining. As mentioned, every other competitor left the mainland USA chasing what they believed were lower costs offshore. It didn't make much sense to us relocating offshore with the extra supply chain expense and time-to-market lengthened so we visited where some of our major competitors were manufacturing.

Relocating to reduce costs by chasing lower labor costs may be necessary to survive, especially when foreign governments subsidize their businesses giving unfair cost advantage. I know two of our competitors were receiving tax advantages by manufacturing in Puerto Rico and the largest competitor was in Europe. Bill Kelly and I took trips researching why our competitors moved offshore and found the federal government tax rules reinforced our competitors to lose jobs in the USA to other countries for cheaper labor costs. This increased the supply chain costs. We wanted to get both lower costs through higher productivity and maintain a lower supply chain cost by not shipping components overseas only to pay to ship finished products back to the USA customers.

In Puerto Rico, there was the additional incentive of Section 936 tax code which allowed companies to reduce their taxes based on employing Puerto Ricans. Jump ahead 25 years and I see the same firms relocating again chasing lower labor costs after this tax rule changed.

Applying the Principles of Transformations

Principle 1: Skill development in problem-solving. This principle is to offer training to all employees and Lincoln did just this and started prior to any thought of the transformation that would start 8 years later. Lincoln also did not stop at training its employees within its walls. Lincoln included training its suppliers.

Quality Circle Problem-Solving was offered to all employees willing to meet for an hour weekly on a problem that the team thought would improve the plant. Quality Circles evolved from Dr. Deming's work and others' who were helping Japan rebuild after World War II. These Quality Circles paved the way for the transformation of the workforce, including the frontline employees who made the products. Lincoln's culture shifted to believing in our employees.

The training in problem-solving was sponsored by the top two leaders, Bill Kelly and Don McCann. They had the foresight to initiate Quality Circles around 1981 to continuously improve Lincoln's manufacturing. The transformation started in the mid-1980s so Bill and Don had already set the transformation preparation into motion. The competitive forces reinforced we needed to retrain our workforce in skills that later supported the transformation efforts.

McGregor[2] made popular Theory X vs. Theory Y management styles. Eaton's leadership training introduced us to this concept. Theory X described a hierarchical command and control culture whereas Theory Y was participative across the levels of organizational structure. Lincoln was already predominantly participative and this facilitated the move to teams solving problems and the Quality Circle teams provided the environment and literally meeting space to train them in problem-solving.

Quality Circle training followed Shewhart's and Deming's scientific methodology for solving problems that focused on root cause analysis and experimenting with solutions. Deming and Shewhart created an acronym for teams to remember the methodology. Plan-Do-Study-Act and a slight twist substituting "Check" for "Study" (PDCA). Plan-Do-Study-Act is a fact-based and data-driven approach fitting well with Lincoln's propensity to require data in everything important from capital acquisition funding requests to the individual incentive pay system.

Quality Circles became popular in Japan and were catching on in America thanks originally to Dr. W. Edwards Deming and Joseph Juran. Deming and Juran assisted Japan in recovering from World War II and Japan gave them credit for transforming Japan's reputation as a poor quality cheap manufacturing country to a world-class competitor. Deming chastised American management for not promoting quality and blaming employees vs. training every employee in quality and problem-solving. Kaoru Ishikawa was the Chief Executive Director of Quality Control Circle Headquarters at the Union of Japanese Scientists and Engineers. He listened to the American quality experts and acted. He developed problem-solving methods, training, and tools including the root cause analysis method. Lincoln was an early USA adopter.

Important to understand is the simplicity of tools in problem-solving and Ishikawa's "7 tools" (shown below in Figure 2.1) proved to solve a vast majority of the issues Lincoln had to solve.

Ishikawa's 7 Tools for Problem-Solving + Productivity

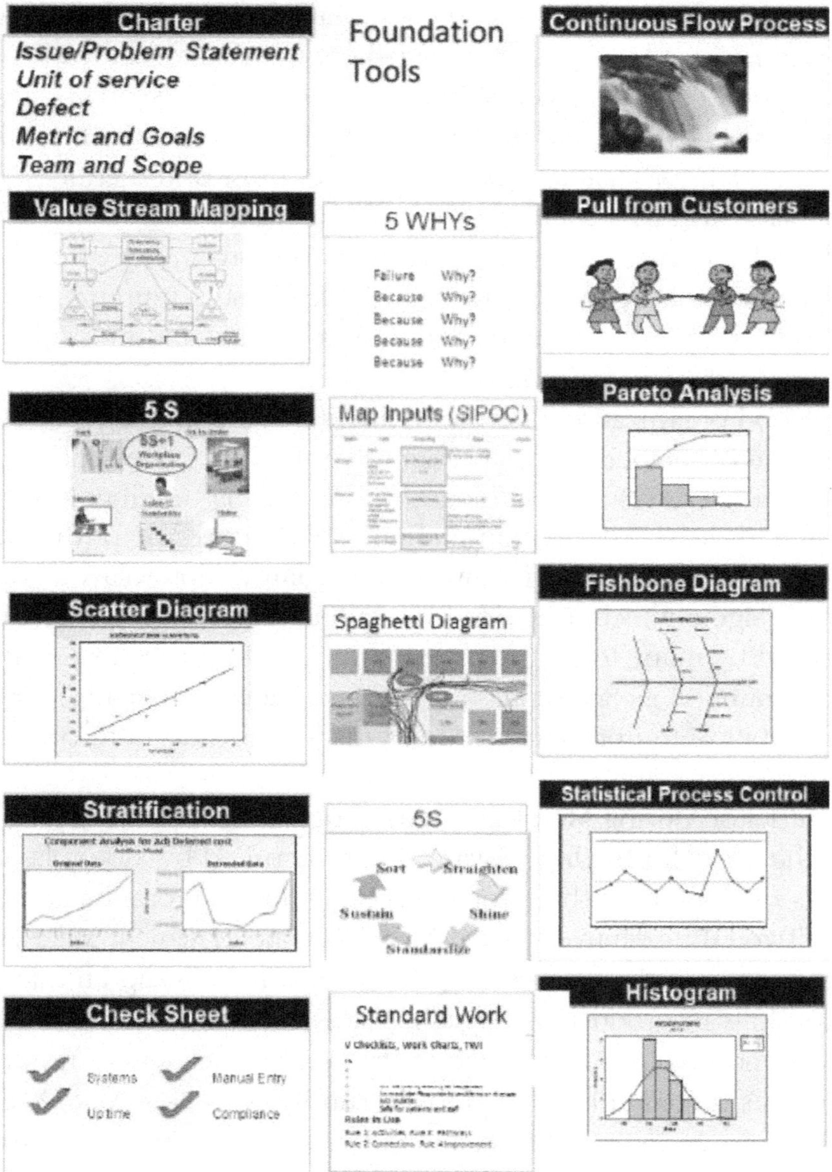

Figure 2.1 Tools taught in team problem-solving. Ishikawa's original seven tools with a few tools from the Toyota Production System and other productivity training.

Lincoln's Quality Circles and the broad training at all levels of the organization paved the way to include them from the very start of the transformation. The Circles and training helped to redesign the flow of Lincoln resulting in moving virtually every machine in this large plant except its biggest punch press and plating lines.

Leadership Training

Beginning before the Quality Circle team training in problem-solving, Lincoln required leadership and management training for all leaders and most managers. This was leadership training to excel, essentially, and was driven by a need to compete in our markets. Lincoln had the typical training sponsored by HR for legal and compliance but most of the effort was training in how to excel as leaders.

Thinking back, there were only two organizations in my career in six large companies that required a program of leadership training in-house other than training in compliance. Eaton was my first and most extensive promoter of leadership training.

The second organization offering problem-solving training was at Motorola where I helped its businesses solve strategic issues and I developed and taught problem-solving building on its Six Sigma training. Motorola is well known for its transformation in quality and being one of the first winners of the US Malcolm Baldrige Award for Quality. Motorola was the birthplace of Six Sigma which it credited for its transformation. Six Sigma training is considered by many to be the premier training for problem-solving. Motorola continued its Six Sigma training and added leadership training in quality, reliability, and productivity as its markets increased in competitive pressures.

I was at Eaton during Motorola's storied transformation in quality and winning the Malcolm Baldrige Award. I was recruited by Motorola as a testament to its ongoing trust that problem-solving training for all is a must to compete. Two GE executives joined Motorola, one of which, Mike Fenger, recruited me to join the Corporate Quality Initiatives Group and develop Motorola's skills in productivity as its markets became even more competitive in cost and quality. Mike is one of the brightest leaders in my career and after I left was recruited by Steve Jobs to run iPhone sales. Mike learned Six Sigma problem-solving and leadership culture at GE in its famous transformation under Jack Welch and his goal was to help Motorola gain back its edge.

Motorola required leadership and management training in quality under Mike's program named, "Quality Vital Signs." Motorola was and continues today to be the market leader in First Responder Communications. In contrast, one business in Motorola had shifted more investment to marketing while deemphasizing the rigor it held in quality and Six Sigma.

When I joined Motorola, it was also the market leader in cellular phones but was losing market share. I'll never forget the day at Motorola where I worked in its corporate headquarters when Apple announced its iPhone. I don't believe it was a coincidence that Motorola's cellular business had put Six Sigma on a back burner, choosing instead to focus on marketing. At the time Motorola was criticized for falling behind in the transition from analog to digital and it wasn't long after I left Motorola that it sold the cellular phone business – a market it co-created with a carrier.

Back to Lincoln. Participative management followed Theory Y practices making Quality Circles and its problem-solving training accepted by most managers. In less participative organizations, middle managers have been known to resist because they felt less secure in their roles when employees have a say and develop ideas to improve their processes.

In 2024, a major union went on strike asking for a 77% pay raise[3] and ceasing efforts to automate. One can understand the motive of the union to save jobs but at what cost? Eaton's Lincoln Plant would probably not exist today if it were not for its transformation and its selective automation that reduced costs of labor and material.

More than likely, competitive, and regulatory pressures may arise over a product's lifetime. A product line's initial capability to meet the market needs may weaken with these additional demands. An example of circuit breakers like those in your home came about with the need in advanced technology to better protect. Ground fault circuit interruption is one such technology that evolved and Eaton had to develop. The design team designed a very capable product line and Lincoln was the one and only manufacturing site. This story includes how a significant product change can transform all product lines. Lincoln built what has been called "electrical safety products" and capability is always about how its products protected buildings and thus people.

Reliability is achieving capability through time. Leading to excel includes achieving the initial capability plus the problem-solving in design and processing problems to continue capability reliably. Design Engineering and Eaton's customers and independent testing organizations, including Underwriters Laboratories (UL) confirmed the capability of our designs before ever being able to sell. Lincoln's manufacturing processes included testing capability every day and we also had UL auditing product capability.

At the ASQ World Conference in 2024, I spoke on reliability and what it took to lead transformations. We found variation and new competitive pressures require continuous problem-solving training and application to maintain reliability. Transformations are improvements that sustained.

Leading to excel incorporates training in how to design products and services as well as the process to make and deliver.

Principle 4: Competitive Strategy

Michael Porter's Five Forces[4] practice explains Eaton's decision to transform the manufacturing and distribution of residential and commercial electrical products made in Lincoln. Competitive Rivalry forced all the major competitors to reduce costs coupled with the bargaining power of customers. The circuit breaker and enclosure proved a viable threat to the industry making electrical fuses. The breaker was a substitute for the simple fuse that was a destructive (one-time use) throw-away safety device.

The circuit breaker allowed the primary function of stopping current to protect a circuit and allowed a homeowner to simply switch the breaker on again. The tripping of the breaker may happen multiple times until the root cause of the overload or short circuit was corrected. Before circuit breakers, one may destroy several fuses while troubleshooting the fault.

Michael Porter's Strategy Forces [See Figure 2.2] concept helps with context why Eaton believed transformative improvement was needed in the 1980s. Michael shares his five forces which may affect a firm's strategy

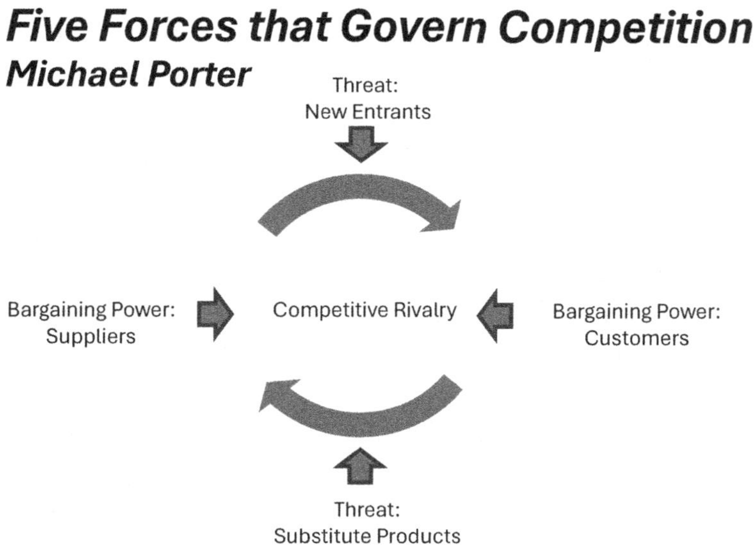

Figure 2.2 Michael Porter, "competitive strategy" and the five forces.

planning. The Bargaining Power of Customers and Competitive Rivalry forces were significant in the electrical distribution safety products.

After the transformation, Lincoln and its customers benefited from a much faster chain from suppliers which shipped only based on when needed vs. a forecast that was always wrong and customers now may receive their products directly from the manufacturing area via truck to the job site. This bypassed the Lincoln finished goods warehouse, shipment to the purchasing electrical distributor, and then to the installing electrician's vehicle. Straight from the Lincoln Plant to the job site was possible. In Figures 2.3 and 2.4

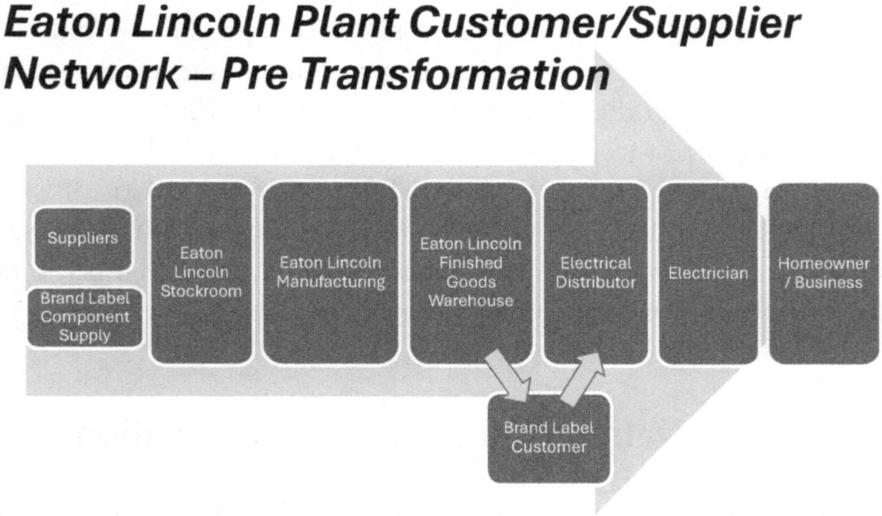

Figure 2.3 Eaton Lincoln Plant customer/supplier network – pre transformation.

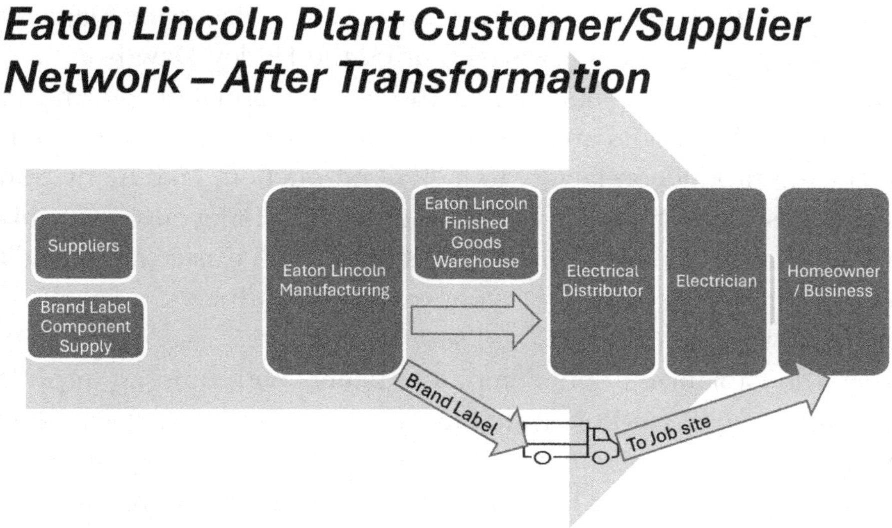

Figure 2.4 Eaton Lincoln Plant customer/supplier network – after transformation.

there are flows of product before and after the transformation. Please refer to these as I describe greater details in this chapter.

Eaton chose a different route than all our competitors. The result can be judged by the Lincoln Plant still operating in 2024. Some products have moved, and new ones have taken their place, but the products that are still manufactured in Lincoln are produced much the same way since the transformation.

An example of a product that left Lincoln is the industrial circuit breaker production. Production moved after a major acquisition consolidating manufacturing resources and Eaton was required to sell the industrial breaker line due to concern about monopolistic advantage. This production did not move to follow lower labor costs. Again, it was government intervention requiring Eaton to sell the product line in the government's thinking we might become a monopoly or to maintain competitors. We could have been pressured to sell to a foreign buyer who may have taken those jobs offshore. Today I wonder if the federal government would have required the sale with its push to bring jobs back. Michael Porter's Five Forces explains the need to consider the forces of government and regulators.

Lincoln's Organizational Structure Transformation

"All the stars aligned" describes the period when Lincoln Plant's organizational structure changed purposely to match the strategy. Principle 5: Engage and Go See Firsthand

Before the transformation, Wayne Boatman, Manufacturing Manager, had interviewed a person who suggested touring the Harley Davidson factory near Milwaukee, WI to see its manufacturing transformation. Wayne, Al, and I drove the four hours and saw how Harley had shifted from a batch manufacturing production facility to a "JIT" production. Like many transformations, it was not just one process that changed. Harley also recognized the cost accounting methods that drove much of the waste in the traditional functionally aligned department layout explained earlier vs. a layout that created better flow in the products and services.

Harley also capitalized on its employee talents with training in problem-solving. Harley mentioned often that its employees were empowered to continuously improve operations. Another sign of Harley's organizational strategy was the use of tour guides who were hourly employees – not the typical management-run tour. Harley's organizational strategy included employees – a major transformation of management/employee relationship especially in this collective bargaining union facility. We had the same situation at Lincoln with a union.

Bill and Don asked us next to arrange a tour of Harley Davidson for our union's leadership. Principle 5: Engage-Go See! The union leaders came back united in our plan to incorporate the employee engagement in its messages to our employees, as well as what we were discussing with our employees.

Prior to the transformation while attending The University of Illinois' Executive MBA Program, I learned in our Operations Research class about cellular flow manufacturing. Kevin Fertig, Director of the MBA Program, mentioned while touring our facility that firms are laying out manufacturing into cellular flow instead of assembly lines and the department layouts Lincoln had. His remarks confirmed that other industries had already made the shift from the way Lincoln had manufactured to a better flow.

While in the MBA program, I authored a paper for Bill and Don which ultimately resulted in the transformation of Lincoln's organizational restructuring which occurred immediately prior to the physical process transformations. I thought organizational design was part of the issue having been a supervisor in the manufacturing area and experienced competing priorities. One such competing priority was to get an electrician or mechanic to come out and fix machinery. Evidently, we were not the priority because we often had to wait for help. It was disturbing when we discovered an electrician was working on someone's light in the office instead of fixing the plastic injection molding machine making parts we needed for customers.

More waste occurred when we asked for an electrician or mechanic because the maintenance department required us to walk a paper request ticket up to the maintenance supervisor's office. "No ticky – no worky" was the process imposed by most service departments including the Tooling department. Organizational redesign done well is not because we had bad people. Redesign addresses the root causes of problems and it is not a "Root Who" analysis. In fact, the head of the maintenance department was one of the best leaders in the plant. Jim, the maintenance manager, had inherited the ticket requirement system. The ticket system wasn't his design at all but one just like many other processes that was, "just the way we do things." During the organizational redesign, Jim became one of the most supportive of the new organizational structure.

The classic manufacturing organization organized people and machines based on function including the services department such as maintenance, toolroom, and all office processes such as material planning and sourcing.

Manufacturing was organized based on the primary function. Stamping metal parts was done in a stamping department. Welding components together was done in a separate welding department. Assembly was in yet a third department. In between these departments there was a stockroom where all incoming parts from suppliers came and all assemblies went back to after a department worked on the parts, only to be moved back out to the manufacturing floor again for final assembly.

Design Engineering led how to transform the design with design for manufacturability key. The Lincoln Plant led the manufacturing and order management transformation. The strategy to compete and stay in the USA also accelerated transforming Lincoln's organizational structure to match the strategy. We needed speed in decision-making to be even faster than the new speed we could take orders, manufacture, and ship any item-any day to beat the competition.

Lincoln was the division's largest facility and housed the largest finished goods warehouse. Most of our competitors did not combine these two very different operations and this unique vertical integration gave us competitive advantage to speed products to market. However, the unique advantages such as speed from production to shipment synergies were not all captured. An example is being able to reduce finished good inventory by increasing the replenishment frequency of the product in the warehouse. Lincoln had lots of finished goods inventory that later would be drastically reduced thanks to the new manufacturing and organizational transformations.

Lincoln's transformation included its most significant organizational structure change in its history. The organizational structure originally was the typical functionally aligned organization. Departments and people would be organized around a function like welding, painting, engineering, and assembly as examples. The transformation in organizational structure came also through studies while I attended the Executive MBA Program at the University of Illinois. As we learned better manufacturing flow, we also explored how organizational structures could be improved. An Operations course I was taking suggested the benefits of transforming the traditional manufacturing layout. Figure 2.5 is an overview of the Lincoln Plant manufacturing layout prior to the transformation. It is at a very high level showing manufacturing and distribution with offices, maintenance and tool departments which were centralized yet served the entire facility, and shipping and receiving. Figure 2.6 zooms in to show the departments within manufacturing. Note that the departments, like maintenance and tooling, were organized by the function. The layout made sense if one wanted to group like

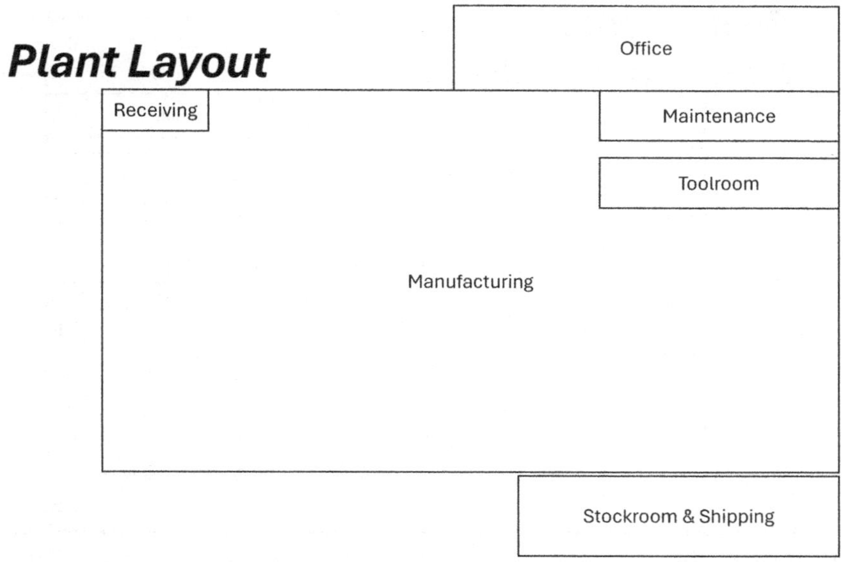

Figure 2.5 Overview of Lincoln layout.

things together. All components made in these departments originated from raw materials from outside the plant or from a central stockroom.

Transforming the Lincoln Plant Structurally

The word transformation may even be an understatement describing how Lincoln changed virtually 100% from the functionally aligned department layout to a Focused Factory layout. [See Figure 2.7] Please refer to this figure throughout this chapter as details are added to the transformation. The Principle 4: Strategize using competitive forces and match organizational structure to strategy resulted in Lincoln shifting entirely from a traditional functional layout and organizational structure to a Focused Factory structure where the layout was organized by product family and flow of the processes to manufacture.

High Level Layout

I was the first Focused Factory Manager and asked to lead the Industrial Breaker product line. This product line included the main breakers installed in the loadcenter Focused Factory so we made and shipped individual breakers to electrical firms and also to our own loadcenter factory. A main breaker is an industrial type breaker you might know as the main breaker in your house. Within the Industrial Breaker product line there were families

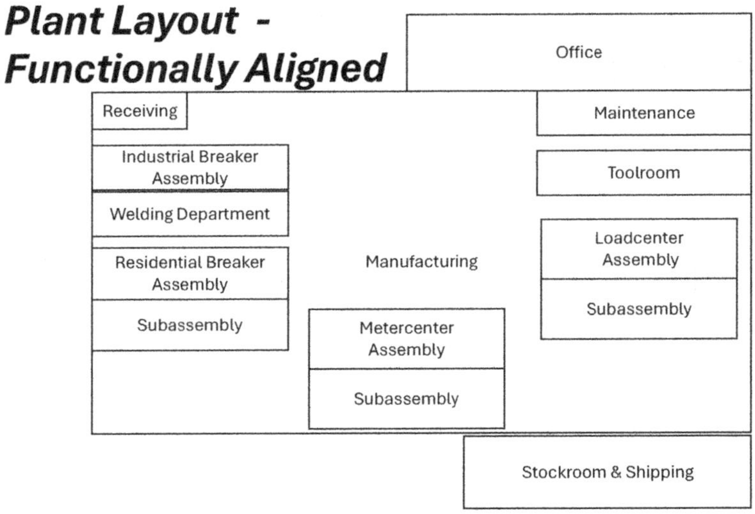

Figure 2.6 Functionally aligned layout.

of products that were different in size and/or function but similar enough to make sense to use the same manufacturing equipment and train employees. Further zooming in shows the manufacturing transformation resulted in cellular flow manufacturing layouts replacing the slow functionally aligned layouts.

Cellular manufacturing organized machines and people into tightly organized areas vs. functionally aligned factories. Instead of all of the welding on components occurring in the welding department as done even in the original Wisconsin plant and Lincoln originally laid out, we literally moved

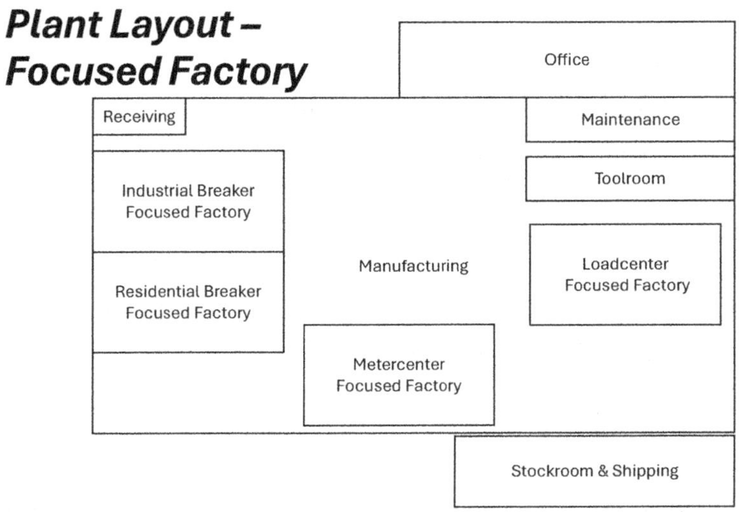

Figure 2.7 Focused factory layout.

the welding machines and people into the assembly area. The product lines became focused factories of product families.

Within the newly created Focused Factories, we created mini factories to produce different major product families. Below is zooming in more to see how one product family was laid out for optimal flow. [See Figure 2.8] This product line made highly customized power panels used in parks where campers would plug their campers into these panels to power their recreational vehicles (RVs). We designed the power panel manufacturing to flow the entire assembly in one cell. We also brought a stamping press into the area to stamp out the cover that could have thousands of permutations based on the customer's wishes. Before the transformation, all stamping presses were in the stamping department. We wanted zero inventory of the covers but we never knew what a customer would order. Now, we could make any cover any day. It was much faster and easier to ask the person skilled in running the stamping press to come to the cell than the old way of putting in a manufacturing order, waiting hours and more often days to get the order to the stamping department and then maybe a week later get it out of the stockroom to the assembly area. With this new focused factory organizational structure and physically co-locating the equipment, we could have any cover any day and within minutes if needed. And zero paperwork which earlier was required to put things into the stockroom and later to get them back out. Organizational structure immediately changed, too. Zero

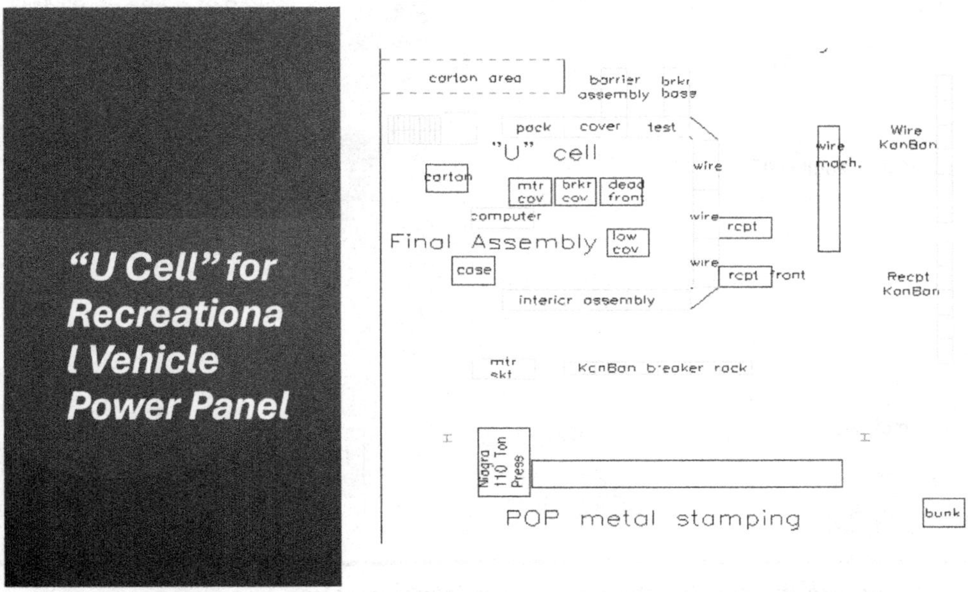

Figure 2.8 U Cell for power outlet panels.

management was involved because the people in the cell were empowered to pull the press operator over to make the covers.

My roles at Lincoln had been in leading Supply Chain, Industrial Engineering, the first Focused Factory, and the Quality Circle Program. I was recruited after graduating to join Eaton at the bottom of the ladder basically to help solve and fix why those large batches of parts the old way manufacturing needed often had missing or the wrong quantity of the right parts sent to the manufacturing areas. The departments could not complete the large batch order because of the wrong parts or wrong quantities were sent from the stockroom. But before this full-time role, I worked at Eaton during college semesters. I learned quickly we behave as we are measured and how leaders reinforced productivity over quality.

[See Figure 2.9] for an overview of how inventory moved before the transformation. Look at all of the movement and one can understand the opportunity to get the parts to the wrong place and in the wrong quantity. The role was to basically inspect the flow and correct errors. This flow is typical of many manufacturers and relies on a central stockroom for parts and components between production steps. We will show the improvement of inventory movement after we cover transformations of reporting and IT which contributed greatly to the transformation.

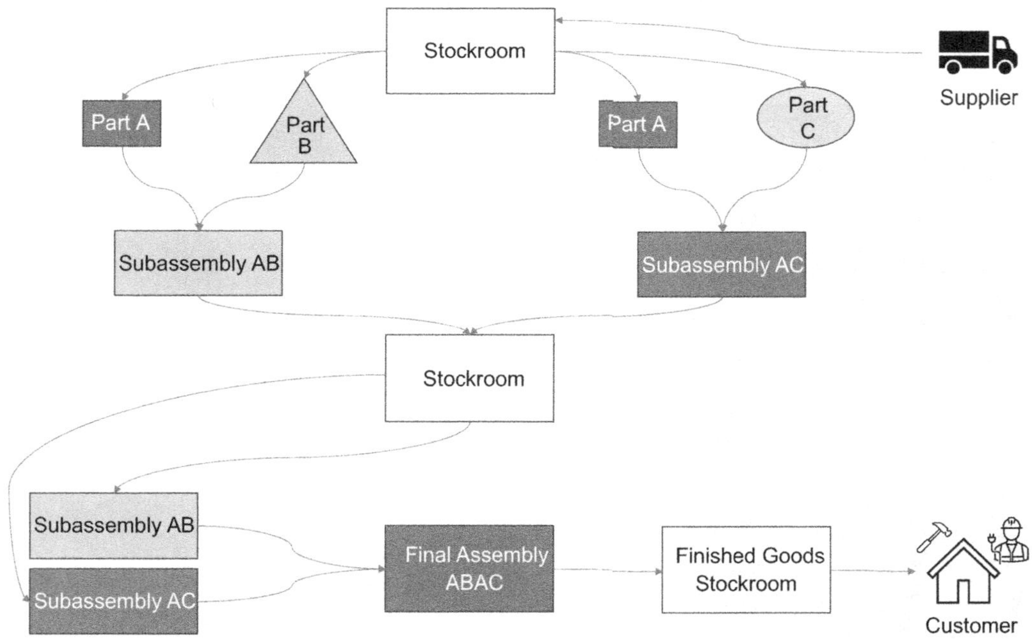

Figure 2.9 Before the manufacturing process transformation.

Transforming Information and Reporting

Lincoln also transformed its Information Technology (IT) including reporting for production and finance. Al Houser was originally hired at Eaton in its Lincoln Plant Finance team. He was promoted to Asheville by John Gilbart, Asheville's plant manager. Asheville made indicator lights and switches not too different in size than Lincoln's circuit breakers. John believed in his managers learning by seeing. He asked Al to spend time on the floor in his first two weeks. The differences between Asheville and Lincoln were obvious, Al said. An example is in how Asheville reported inventory movement. Asheville was the only plant doing backflush vs. transacting each use. I detail backflush later in the chapter for those interested. Lincoln would manually report every component moved to another department. Using the backflush method, the IT system would automatically transact movement knowing the component would have been used in an assembly. The assembly was simpler at Asheville but still very similar so what Al learned in Asheville served us well in Lincoln.

Asheville backflushed everything. Some standard products and some products were special orders due to unique customer requirements. Asheville had no people scheduling what was to be made in manufacturing. Lincoln had schedulers scheduling all manufacturing.

Supervisors were in charge of making sure the right things were done in Asheville. Asheville wanted nothing in stock and had transformed its manufacturing and information flow to accomplish this. This was a shift that Lincoln also accomplished from the old way of having everything in the stockroom with an onhand balance showing in reports. This lack of a stockroom and onhand amount upset Milwaukee distribution because Milwaukee staff felt more comfortable seeing the amount of inventory. Transformations often involve other organizations and success is often "selling" the changes. The principle to go-see works well to help others see and offering outside organizations to become a part of the changes. Lincoln used this often to get suppliers to shift to a more Just In Time process.

Al learned at Eaton's Asheville Plant about simplifying reporting of material movement and benefits of a "JIT" model of manufacturing. Just-In-Time means that production made product soon when the customer wanted it. Many manufacturing sites instead produced what a forecast order was written for and then product was stored waiting for a customer to want it. Inventory was significantly more than in a JIT production facility and often slow to react when the customer wanted products different than what the customer wanted.

John hired Al because he wanted someone in between manufacturing and IT. Gilbart would meet Al at 5 AM and Al shared it was not uncommon for John and Al to find a way to improve information and John would do the reprogramming, test it, and start producing. Agile is an IT term based on manufacturing's Just In Time methods. For those who know the software methodology named, "Agile," Gilbart lived being agile with software development. He could make changes after leaving a meeting, check if it works, and put the improvement into production. As an aside, I have been in organizations claiming to have utilized agile methods which were nothing close to Just In Time. In fact, I found the IT changes extremely slow and too much time spent in planning and saying no to users because users' requests can't mess up the plan created weeks ago. This so-called IT agile is the exact opposite of agility - being able to quickly take new requests and produce any item any day.

IT orders were similarly as complex and as slow as the manufacturing order system. Al eliminated IT orders as we did with maintenance and tooling requests. In Lincoln, we had to submit an IT request, then the request sat at the IT manager's desk, and then maybe it would get assigned and accomplished.

Pete Krol, General Manager of Asheville and Lincoln, got to know Al while Al was at Asheville. Pete wanted Al to help Lincoln improve operations after seeing Asheville's successes. Al was promoted to the Lincoln Plant as its Controller to jumpstart Lincoln's improvement.

Al after returning to Lincoln and having the IT department report to him in his CFO role, shifted to have an "Appetite for Speed." This same hierarchical and slow ticket system was found in getting maintenance and tooling work done. Al called this order system, "King of the hill roadblock." Whoever was deemed more important than others got their "Order" sooner.

The first improvement was redesigning the daily and monthly reporting. Eventually all of the financial debits and credits were automated. Before these transactions were done manually. At month-end close, aka EOM, staff manually entered them and then wasted time by mailing them to Milwaukee HQ.

IT got the daily transaction report going so we could see it earlier. This improved onhand balance accuracy. Journal entry was automated and End of Month accounting routine was done in a day. This speed also improved quality. Al could catch an error because the report did not balance. Al likes to, "Ask why five times" and finds it is a good practice to solve problems and a simple principle 1 – Develop skills in problem-solving.

The Lincoln Plant was ready for a transformation in manufacturing reporting, too. The financial system and controller had a lot of power. Not too many organizations or people in the Lincoln Plant were interested in backflushing at this time. Al always thought we could backflush at shipment.

Principle 2 – Utilize Measure, Manage to the measure, and Making it easier (3Ms) gave us the glidepath for the transformation. Al Houser led improving the measuring, managing, and making it easier for financial and manufacturing reporting.

Lincoln's transformation capitalized on data analytics skills that Al Houser had and some of his IT team members had. Their work resulted in better dashboards than many organizations have today even with today's dashboard applications. Al and the IT team transformed the reporting available to leaders and what would eventually be visible to all employees. One important example is how they were able to display near real-time KPIs including productivity rates, the day's sales, and inventory on every computer screen.

How many organizations today only see their key measures monthly if not quarterly? Data and measures were so important that Al and team developed a way that no one could miss the important data and scores of successes. They transformed reporting to display key metrics at the first sign-on every day. Not only did reports come without effort, but the scoreboard also popped up automatically and before the employee could enter any other computer application. No one could NOT see the KPI status. The digital display available on every computer monitor was also much better than the printed reports that could only be seen by the one person who had the report. The digital display also brought the information faster for all to see. And this was on an IBM central system without PCs. Today's IT systems are so much easier and still few organizations have access to its KPIs as well as Lincoln had in the 1980s.

The KPIs vital to Lincoln's success were now on a well-designed easy-to-read dashboard. Lincoln, starting with its Quality Circles, was becoming a highly participative culture with many hourly employees also having access to the reporting. Every Quality Circle Leader had access to help problem-solving teams know key measures needing improvement and how their solutions worked. These frontline employees in turn shared with their colleagues and facilitated many more teammates managing to the measures and focusing teams in making work easier. This kept a focus on the customer and the strategy to speed products at lower cost.

Al Houser drove utilizing the 3Ms as the Controller but also as the leader of the IT organization. The IT group facilitated sharing key measures so all could and would manage to the measures. Making it easier to know status is an important aspect of making it easier. Later we will see how we made it easier in our core mission of serving customers.

When Al returned to Lincoln he found, "Lincoln was way, way, way too complicated." Al believed, "you don't fix it a piece at a time." Al fed this view back to the Plant Manager Bill Kelly and to Pete that Lincoln was so complex only a "transformation" would allow Lincoln to compete in this highly competitive industry with many players.

You have seen production systems similar to how Lincoln and many manufacturers planned production. You have seen a fast food restaurant that has different chutes based on sandwich versions. Sandwiches are made in advance waiting on a customer to order. As you walk up to order, the cooks are busy making sandwiches that someone thought customers would want. And they make the same sandwich in batches hoping what they are cooking is what you want.

You walk up and order a sandwich but what you want is not in any chute. So, you either wait for what you really want or change your order to something already made in the chute. My analogy after the transformation is being able to make whatever you order just in time and eliminate many of the burgers in the chutes. Tell me you never changed your order to what a chute had so you did not have to wait. Is that great customer service?

Manufacturers often planned production in large lots and hoped these large stocks sitting in a warehouse would sell. The cost accounting mindset contributed to making large batches due to individual part costing. The setup time before the next product could be manufactured was assigned to each piece-part and could significantly change what the cost accounting system calculated the "cost" of making a part. The cost accounting practice was to allocate the overhead cost of downtime of changing over processes to each batch of product. The larger the batch (denominator), seemingly the lower the cost to manufacture. If a setup took two hours, that cost of labor and overhead is allocated over 10,000 parts vs. a few thus making one part look much cheaper. Much of the fixed overhead is exactly that – it is fixed and does not change based on the quantity of parts made.

What Asheville and Lincoln experienced with the large batch manufacturing practices was plenty of inventory, but not the right inventory. Adding to the aggravation in supply chain and manufacturing for working on products no one bought and not having products customers wanted was Lincoln's customer service department, who had to address customers who wanted something different. The large batches tied up resources and prevented these same resources from making what the customer wanted.

Al and the IT team made the measuring and managing to the measures easier. Making reporting easier made it easier for Lincoln to know what to measure including better costing of products. Better cost information made it easier for my team when I led Industrial Engineering to focus on the biggest productivity improvements. We would measure more important variables such as group productivity – not individual and thus better manage to these better measures vs. wasting time on measures that are not only not that important, but some measures like individual incentive were also dysfunctional. Next I explain my career within Eaton to better explain the transforming of how we paid employees and the dysfunctionality.

Transforming Pay – Individual Incentive Piece-Part system

The piece-part incentive system added to the frustration of inventory problems. The majority of employees on the frontline assembling product were eligible for extra pay. Imagine being able to make 125% or more over base salary and not having the parts to earn the incentive? This happened often and I lived it while working on the frontline between college semesters.

I remember being able to make my quota early in the day, running out of parts, and then trying to find something to build even if not needed so I could earn more money. This was dysfunctional because inventory is waste. The money spent results in no income if sitting waiting to be sold. I, and my colleagues, were incentivized to build despite not needing what I was building. One may wonder why management would provide other work even when the day's quota was met.

Incentive pay was dysfunctional in achieving lower cost and speeding product delivery to customers. It reinforced quantity over quality resulting in defective products which required rework of pallets of nonconforming material. There were also tricks employees learned that had nothing to do with improving products but sure improved their take home pay. A coworker taught me that the screw I was told to put in to hold an inner cover was not needed to be installed. Just throw it in the box because, and this made sense, the electrician has to remove the screw and cover to wire the enclosure. Made sense to me and earned me more incentive pay. One day an inspector took a product off the pallet of products I made, shook one can, and discovered the loose screw trick. He rejected the load.

What was even more dysfunctional was I still got the incentive pay. But it gets crazier. Another person in the rework area, yes there was a rework area, fixed what I did wrong. But still worse, this person who repaired everything also got incentive.

The answer is understood by using the adage, "we behave as we are measured." Supervisors were measured on productivity – a KPI. It is the ratio of production/hours. Production was measured in standard hours of credit that the operation should take times the number of parts sent to the stockroom divided by the attendance hours. Management, too, was incentivized to keep me and everyone building something so they would get credit for shipping components or finished goods into the stockroom. Oh, and let's not forget the mirage of lowered costs by absorbing fixed overhead based on volume. Again, into the stockroom – not to a customer.

Al and I made this dysfunctional incentive pay system one of the most important reasons a transformation was needed. Many employees earned 20% or more above base pay and to change their pay would be highly emotional. Quality was truly the most important measure in these electrical products. Safety was never compromised and the individual incentive pay system had to be eliminated – not just tweaked. Jim Campbell, head of Quality, and Wayne Boatman, Manufacturing Manager agreed despite 20+ years of having the incentive system. The transformation made it possible.

As manager of Industrial Engineering prior to being named the Industrial Breaker Focused Factory Manager, we too measured labor productivity. My Industrial Engineers were responsible for improving manufacturing productivity and this began with measuring productivity. Measuring productivity began with the individual production worker and in fact focused on the individual more so than the manufacturing group. This focus on the individual will be completely upended in the transformation.

We managed to the individual measure by helping the production areas improve processes and we often worked with design engineering to make it easier to make the products. As mentioned earlier, Lincoln had an individual piece-work incentive system based on measuring the time it took individuals to make a quantity of products. An Industrial Engineer's role was consumed measuring, managing to the measure, and making it easier for production to make products. Individuals were reinforced to make as many products as possible in the shortest time and their pay increased. We saw how measuring individual incentives can drive the wrong behaviors and how Lincoln's transformation radically changed how it measured labor productivity. But we had to change the flow of orders to a JIT flow vs. the huge wasteful batches that allowed individuals to stay on a task long enough to earn incentive.

The materials replenishment system was transformed from a manufacturing order being required to order parts from suppliers, then an order to stock the parts, and then another order to "Push" the parts from the stockroom to the assembly areas. Oh yes, and yet another order needed created to store the finished goods in a finished goods warehouse.

The transformation replaced the push system with a Pull system explained earlier to replenish the parts based simply on consumption – not some computer-generated order which was wrong in quantity and timing. Walking through the plant before the transformation one would see lots of activity of parts being made but the parts would soon disappear into a huge stockroom based on the order created from a forecast.

Later, these same parts would be pulled to fill an order by stockroom personnel and sent back to the manufacturing area again for more work.

The new Pull system and flowing subassemblies within the final assembly "U-shaped" cell eliminated subassembly inventory in many product lines and also eliminated the need to stock expensive final assemblies. Best yet is Lincoln achieved record high on-time performance to customers.

The transformation eliminated all the movements back to the stockroom until the final product was ready to ship to customers or a finished goods warehouse. Lincoln was also the business' largest warehouse for its products and afforded Lincoln's transformation an even bigger impact we will discuss.

In Figure 2.10, one can see the vastly simpler flow the transformation achieved. Remember I was hired to help solve why the large batches of parts ordered from the stockroom often were incorrect. Although I was grateful for this first job, I enjoyed eliminating the causes that resulted in Don and Bill hiring me in the first place. The transformed order system, essentially the elimination of the orders, eliminated the movement of parts to a stockroom by creating a flow of functions within the same geographic area. All the excess movement of parts was no longer happening so we also transformed by reducing the information required to run Lincoln.

As factory manager after the transformation, my frontline staff and supervisors simply watched the prior day's production quantity go down and the next day we built to replace what was consumed. No manufacturing order was now needed. Most of the complexity was eliminated in forecasting, entering orders in large batches into the computer, printing those orders for the manufacturing areas, sending the orders to the stockroom to pick the parts for those orders, and finally delivering the parts from the stockroom to

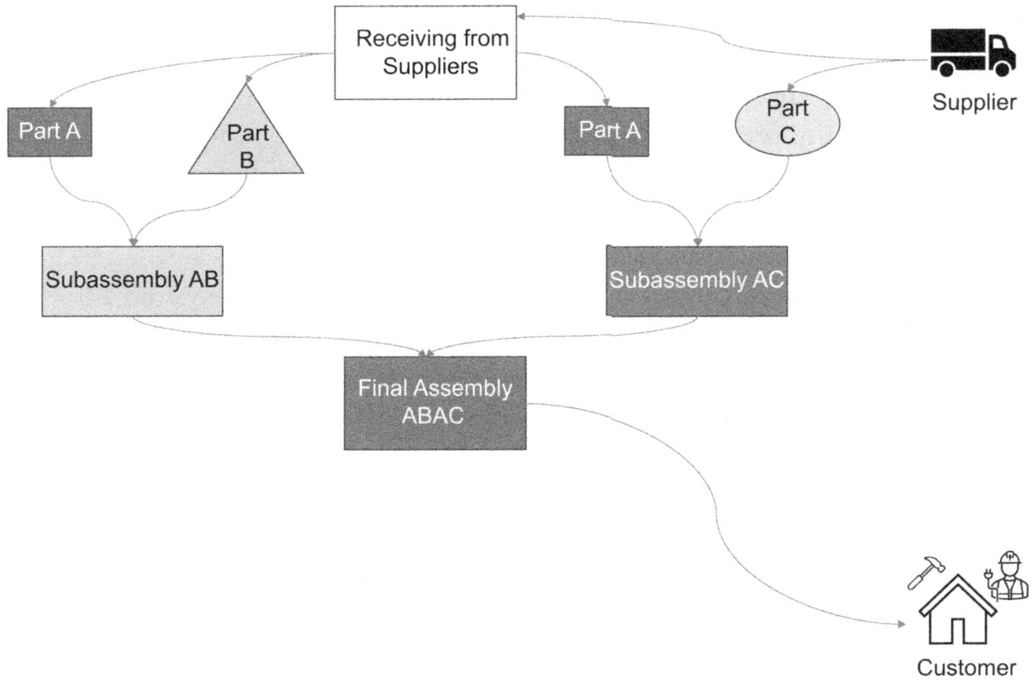

Figure 2.10 After the transformation product flow simplified.

the area where they were needed to produce product. After the transformation, if a part was only used in one area, Lincoln eventually only stored the part in that area. Even if used in multiple areas, there was only one master storage location, and a paper card (Kanban as often referred to in JIT) was used to replenish the smaller usage areas. No orders needed at all.

The first kanban, Al remembers, was started when the departments had many places they shoved parts. Al said we need one spot to stock it and everyone could find what they were looking for. Dwayne Jensen, Stockroom Manager and IT professional, was helpful in finding a permanent spot for each component for the kanban location. Al added it has to be visually organized so you can't mess it up.

Another waste eliminated was the reporting to ensure incentive pay was accurate. This consumed hours and hours of staff time. Customers couldn't care less about these transactions, but they sure cared how much we had to add to our price to pay for these wastes.

The transformation was partially driven by the incentive pay system's driving of excess production, shortages of products, and sometimes poor quality. Incentive inhibited teamwork. Anyone earning incentive was reinforced to not share how because, "If I can find a way to do it better, why would I tell anyone and that trigger the Industrial Engineers to change the standard?" Individual incentive piecework reinforced many employees to not share ideas. What Lincoln needed was teamwork and we knew our employees were filled with ideas to improve.

Al and I calculated the overall productivity for the first time – we had a new KPI. Then, I took the individual incentive payout to calculate the average incentive earned. Al and I calculated what overall productivity had to improve to breakeven by eliminating the individual incentive pay. This amount was given to Bill and Don who achieved agreement with the union to cease the individual incentive pay. Nearly everyone benefited because Don and Bill agreed to increase the base wages of every union employee essentially the amount we paid on incentive. So, instead of paying some of the employees individual incentive pay and Eaton incurring all the wasted costs of excess inventory and rework caused by rushing for quantity, all employees benefited. We believed our employees would not only maintain overall productivity without the individual incentive pay, but with all the transformation improvements, we made it easier for them to produce and productivity would improve. We were proven correct. The new KPI measuring productivity at a factory level with ALL employees improved compared to the years under individual incentive pay. All labor was in the new productivity KPI, too including material handling, inspection, maintenance, tooling, and eliminated the individual incentive pay system. Productivity is the number one KPI for labor manufacturing and verified the transformation success. Celebrating team success across the plant was a delightful change from an individual seeing his or her weekly incentive pay while most staff were not even eligible for extra pay they now received under this new plan.

Quality also improved once we switched to this overall productivity reporting and displayed the KPI to all employees. No more incentive for tricks like leaving screws loose, hurry up and make mistakes, and paying incentive to rework. Best yet, the Quality Circles now started working on projects to improve quality instead of projects that helped them make higher incentive pay.

Transforming How Inventory Was Measured

Lincoln was reporting movement of a part multiple times as it moved into and out of the stockroom as work on the product progressed in manufacturing departments. Al's vision was to report only once, twice at the most. Customers don't care a bit about how we tracked inventory and they certainly don't want to pay for it. So, we worked to eliminate this wasted time.

Lincoln received material from the supplier and reported the receipt. Every time that same part moved to a new area, we reported it again. Al envisioned only reporting receiving it and reporting it leaving to the customer as a sellable final product. "Everything (reporting inventory movement) in between is a joke," Al said. All a plant needs to know what it brings in. A "D20" was the name of the transaction the receiving department created by reporting the amount of product received. The D20 was not even being used to pay the supplier. Lincoln was using the actual paper invoice to pay. The invoice is often going to be inaccurate because the quantity the supplier said was shipped was different. An accounting person would try to match the receipt and D20 quantity reported every day.

Lincoln also had a transaction to report the quality of the supplier's shipment. We needed to know if we got the right parts and the right quantity. This "D19" transaction triggered someone in the Quality department to accept the load. Basically, this suggests the Quality department performed a receiving inspection of materials on every receipt from suppliers. Despite this inspection step that slowed materials from being received and being processed, Lincoln found defectives when the parts made it to the manufacturing area. Receiving inspection was another task that was transformed. The transformation was based on Dr. W. Edwards Deming's coaching that inspection is not reliable to ensure quality. The D19 transaction was worthless and added to the complexity of measuring. Al posed we just need to know what came in and what went out.

What drove the material transaction reporting was the physical movement of materials. Every part went from the front of the plant to the back of the plant to the stockroom only to be pulled back into the plant every time a manufacturing order was made to add more value to a part. An example is a part that may need to be welded to another part. After welding, this subassembly of two parts would move back to the stockroom with a transaction needed. Later, the subassembly would move back to manufacturing to be plated and returned to the stockroom once again. Then, we had another transaction to come out of the stockroom and yet another transaction when the part came back after welding.

Al also questioned why Lincoln continued to have a planning group to plan a manufacturing order for every single activity in every department and all based on a forecasted need – not on actual demand. In other words, nothing started in manufacturing without an order created by the planning department and this order also triggered the storeroom to send parts to the manufacturing area. Al gave a vision of manufacturing without any internal production order. What needed to be manufactured would be based on customer orders and not a forecast of the planning department's guessing what customers might need.

Transforming Knowing What to Make When

The first Focused Factory was my factory making Industrial Breakers. Instead of producing what a forecasted manufacturing order wanted, my team started producing many of the plant's highest volume items every day in the quantity shipped out the prior day. While I led transforming the layout of the focused factory and coaching our Industrial Engineers in charge of transforming the other focused factories, Al led transforming information systems.

The Focused Factory Layout opened doors to push decision-making down to the frontline. Decentralizing the decision-making from front office staff to sometimes the union frontline employees created a great need to change the information flow. The improved speed achieved by the Focused Factories and decentralized decision-making put a demand on information keeping up. Operations needed to make the product and Al delivered much better and faster information to the Focused Factories. Manufacturing teams now had what the customer ordered, status of parts, what was consumed, and key information when the customer wanted the product. We measured, managed in real time to the measure, and made the processes easier.

For the high volume products that we knew would be consumed, we set a daily flow rate and watched the inventory to just make sure a peak or trough in demand did not result in a need to change the rate of daily production. Taking out the variability caused by forecasted shop order demands within our factory also dramatically improved what the supplier was seeing in our demand. This "Pull" system vs. the "Push" system transformed not only our manufacturing it also transformed our suppliers by us smoothing our demand for their products. Pull refers to the customer buying product and we then "pulled parts" to replace what our customers ordered (consumed.) Pushing refers to production orders based on a forecast "pushing" production hoping customers want the products made from these parts pushed into manufacturing. We stopped using planned orders to know what to build and simply replaced daily what we sold the day before and we made the highest volume items every day.

The 80/20 rule to know which items were high volume worked in knowing what to build in the Industrial Breaker factory as well as the other focused factories. Lincoln used this rule to make it easier to manufacture what customers needed and benefited in eliminating 100% of the manufacturing orders. I don't know how precise the 80/20 rule fit but Lincoln's product catalog included thousands of products whose demand were very low. We smoothed the entire production by making high volume products often and reserving time every day to make the low volume products. No more large batches tying up resources allowed us to "switch on a dime." In the largest physical focused factory, residential and commercial loadcenters, just four products amounted to 80% of the resources. In residential circuit breakers, 15 amp and 20 amp branch breakers, those breakers most homeowners see in their homes, were by far the most demanded breakers. The same for the industrial breaker line which produced mainly the 200 amp and 100 amp breakers because these breakers were often installed in the high volume loadcenters before leaving the factory.

Lincoln was more advanced in utilizing the 3Ms than most organizations in my career. Yet, we needed to take it to a whole new level to compete. Lincoln, as well as many manufacturing and distribution sites, are experts at measuring. Some industries reinforce measurement better than others, too.

Electrical safety devices are measured by not only by those who make the products but also by regulatory agencies. The same for the healthcare industry as I will share in Chapter 6.

Underwriters Laboratories (UL) provides independent testing and certification that circuit breaker manufacturers comply with UL standards for safety. Unlike some industries like financial services and healthcare, electrical safety product manufacturing was not directly regulated by the federal government. The markets Eaton sold to valued compliance to UL requirements and thus reinforced Eaton and our competitors to comply to UL standards. We valued having UL recognition for our products and it was of value unlike much of the ISO burden I detail in this book.

Two of the four focused factories made circuit breakers. A KPI in circuit breaker function is the time to trip when a fault occurs. The two major fault scenarios are short circuits and overloads. The measure of capability and reliability is the time the circuit breaker takes to trip when a fault occurs. A direct short example is when an extension cord is crushed and the hot and neutral wires touch. UL and Eaton measure how long it takes the breaker in milliseconds to trip and thus mitigate the risk of fire. An overload fault is a more common fault and occurs when the energy flowing through the circuit is greater than the wire and devices are designed to handle. An example is when we put a toaster and a crock pot and too many other devices on the same circuit. The key performance measure is how long it takes to trip.

Managing to that measure is the most important measure because failure to manage to the measure may result in a product failing to function. This in turn may result in a shutdown of sales and expensive recalls in this safety devices. Making it easier to achieve the "Time to trip" is an example of utilizing two of the three Ms, Measure and Manage to the measure. Making it easier was a big win from the easier flow, reporting, and cellular flow without all the waste of inventory movement and transactions.

After the Transformation

The transformation improved every one of the thousands of products Lincoln made. The Wall Street Journal published a story of Lincoln's transformation after Eaton's Sandy Cutler highlighted Lincoln's record high productivity, employee satisfaction, on-time delivery, and his recognition of Lincoln being one of the top plants worldwide.

Transforming the Organization

The first Focused Factory was the Industrial Breaker Factory. Sandy Vinyard was the materials planner assigned from the central planning group to our first factory. She jumped in with both feet transforming inventory supply from the Manufacturing Resource Planning (MRP) system methods utilizing a forecast to one based simply on replenish what was used.

This new way of replenishing the manufacturing area with the component parts it needed to produce the breakers was a "Pull" system vs. the former way which "pushed" component parts best on a best guess forecast of what breakers would be needed by customers. Instead of a computer calculating the amount of components needed to build the breakers planned, Sandy and the team determined a small quantity of each part and stored 100% of the parts where the assembly would occur.

The diagram below illustrates the before and after locations of components and the key departments which made components for the industrial breaker. A location was also simplified for the industrial breakers to be installed in loadcenters. [See Figures 2.11, 2.12] Realize that the same Pull system was occurring at the circuit breaker finished goods level. Instead of a computer-generated order to produce breakers, the breaker focused factory now simply built what was bought.

The suppliers shipped raw materials or components to Lincoln to make component parts. This same Pull system vs. forecasted purchase order was

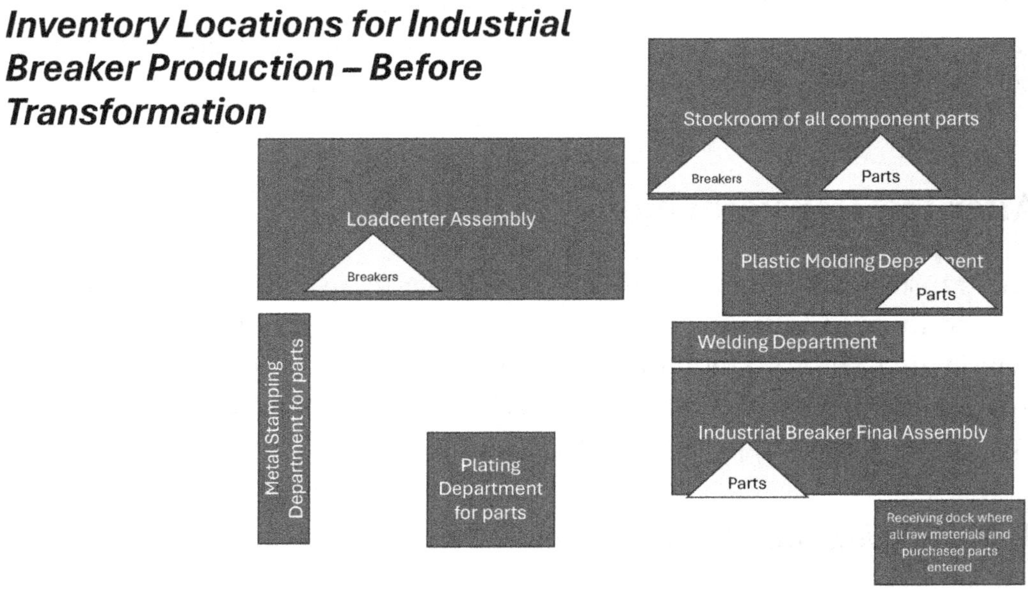

Figure 2.11 Traditional stocking of components in a stockroom.

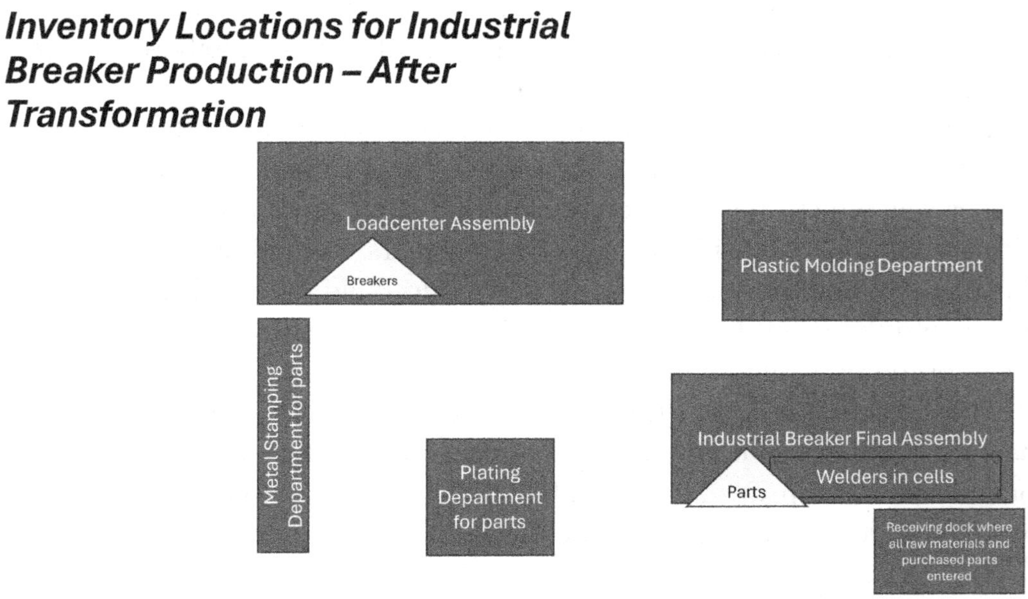

Figure 2.12 After the transformation with point-of-use stocking.

how our focused factory "Bought" from suppliers. The entire supply chain was transformed.

Point-of-use stocking of every component among the thousands required to make industrial breakers in the Industrial Breaker Focused Factory replaced the stockroom entirely. An industrial breaker is typically larger than the breaker some have in the home that they reset when a circuit trips. The industrial breaker is the main breaker and thus the Lincoln Focused Factory produced breakers for individual sales and supplied Lincoln's other Focused Factory which produced loadcenters when a main breaker is required. The individual sales and internal use allowed our first Focused Factory to see improvement quickly.

The triangles represent inventory of component parts or raw materials needed in the assembly of an industrial breaker. The departments are those that were key to producing the components.

Once the Pull systems began, the entire stockroom storing the components and raw materials was no longer needed. Parts purchased from outside suppliers went directly from the receiving dock to where the parts would be assembled into breakers. Before the Pull system, the receiving dock would move 100% of the parts to the stockroom, which required staff to put the parts on a shelf only to be later picked from those shelves and delivered to the industrial breaker assembly areas.

The Pull system allowed Lincoln to redeploy the stockroom people out to the areas that produced product. And this eliminated capital requirements including fork trucks used primarily to move parts into and out of the stockroom only to end up where they were needed for assembly into the final products.

Transformations like Lincoln's also transformed the mindset of employees. Employees had more control and autonomy with the Pull system because they turned in the kanban cards and knew firsthand what was ordered and what to expect. The push system was managed by people in the front office and the employees on the floor often would wonder why they were getting parts from the stockroom when what the customer needed them to build did not require the parts pushed onto them.

Principle 7 – Celebrate Quick Wins

Celebrating came early and often as employees gained more control over their work. Another benefit was the management of orders now came directly to some of the production cells vs. through a management staff person as all orders were delivered before the transformation. Employees celebrated seeing the right parts when they needed them throughout the day instead of running out of needed parts and relying on management to solve the shortage issues and often to find out what the computer plan called for.

Besides having the right inventory, seeing the inventory wastes reduced by the employees putting the parts where they needed them and just the amount they needed was celebrated by teams across the plant who implemented the kanban Pull system.

I have been in organizations where leaders are so vain to think they must be the hosts to celebrations. Celebrating does not need management. A celebration only when management is the giving party is insulting to adults. Employees gained pride in seeing results. Sure, we in leadership participated in some planning of more formal celebrations, but the employees didn't need us to celebrate.

Principle 2: Utilizing the 3Ms: Measure, Manage to the Measure, and Make it Easier Guided the Transformation

In Measure, SMART goals included the days-on-hand of inventory. Now every employee could see the inventory instead of searching for a computer to see what the stockroom had and experience employees could estimate the days-on-hand knowing how many they would consume in a day. So, the SMART goal was to reduce the days-on-hand from months, if not years, to days and some parts were down to hours of inventory.

SMART goals always included on-time ship performance and the fill rate. Fill rate is usually calculated as the % of demand with enough inventory to ship on-time. These two measures cover 100% of the orders because some products are expected to be in stock and some orders are build-to-order and not stocked. After the transformation, every employee had access to the prior day's performance in these two KPIs. And, Lincoln started measuring a proxy to "Received on-time" which is what the customer really cares about. The Industrial Breaker factory prior to me leading it was months behind in orders promised to customers. Within months we eliminated the backorder and eventually reduced the amount of finished breakers stored in regional warehouses because we could build any item any day and thus "safety stocks" were not needed.

Safety stocks were a fudge factor for inaccurate forecasts and/or delays in Lincoln production. The reliability of production getting the right breaker when needed allowed some safety stocks to be eliminated entirely. The loadcenter demand for industrial breakers was steady and allowed 100% of the breakers to move directly from the breaker assembly cell to the loadcenter cells needing the breakers.

Principle 4 – Competitive Strategy: Transforming at the Customer

Our strategy to compete on speed and lower cost led to major advances in competitive advantage. This strategy also helped transform some major customers. Lincoln continues today benefitting from this next story of transforming Eaton and one of its largest customers.

Lincoln made metering enclosures like the ones on multifamily housing and commercial buildings. We also brand labeled for a well-known company that pioneered the electrical industry. The customer used the same push system to order from us the metering products they needed and we would build and ship them to their warehouses. The problem both we and the customer had was the customer often ordered what it did not need for its customers and did not order products it needed.

We proposed applying the same cellular flow manufacturing and pull system in building its products and receiving and shipping its orders. Instead of the same push order to fill the customer's finished goods warehouses in hopes its customers wanted the inventory, we asked them to give us the order it got from its customers. At the time, the client was manufacturing and distributing just like Eaton did. This transformation story will hit home with many and sadly most manufacturing companies because "everybody" was doing it like Eaton did. Large companies, primarily, have the money to waste. No one would run a small business like this, I hope.

The client would forecast what its customers wanted months in advance. [See Figure 2.13] Then it batched this demand into a purchase order for Eaton. This purchasing order was received and then Eaton made a manufacturing order and may change quantities and dates to meet our wishes, which resulted in Eaton having the waste of the client's brand-labeled expensive finished goods. Finally, a stockroom order would be sent to the stockroom to pick and send to the manufacturing areas enough parts to make our

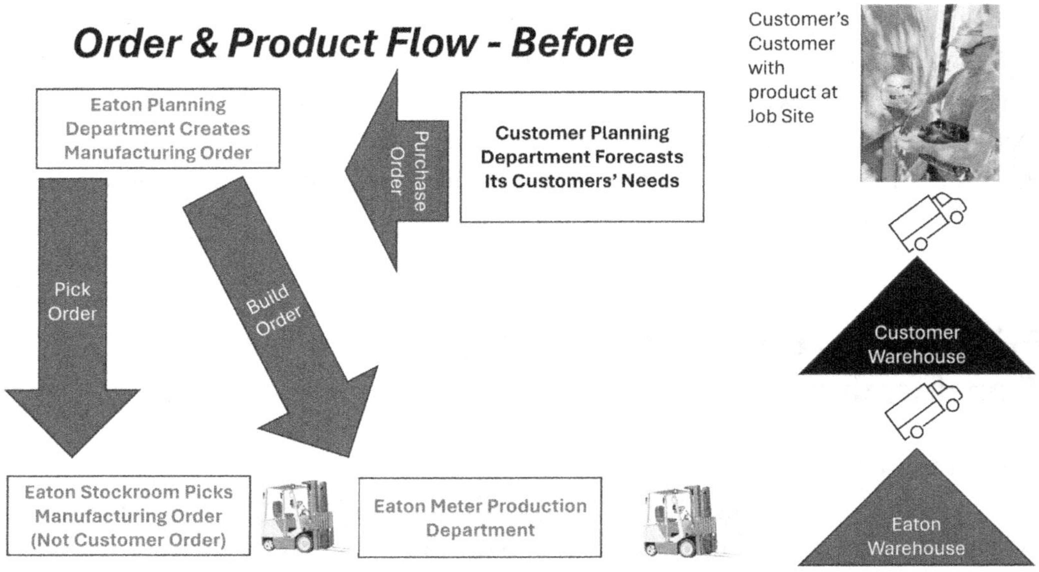

Figure 2.13 Order flow before transformation.

manufacturing order, to fill the customer's order to Eaton, to fill its warehouse with finished products that the customer thought its customers might want.

A picture is worth a thousand words so below is what the order process looked like after the transformation. [See Figure 2.14]

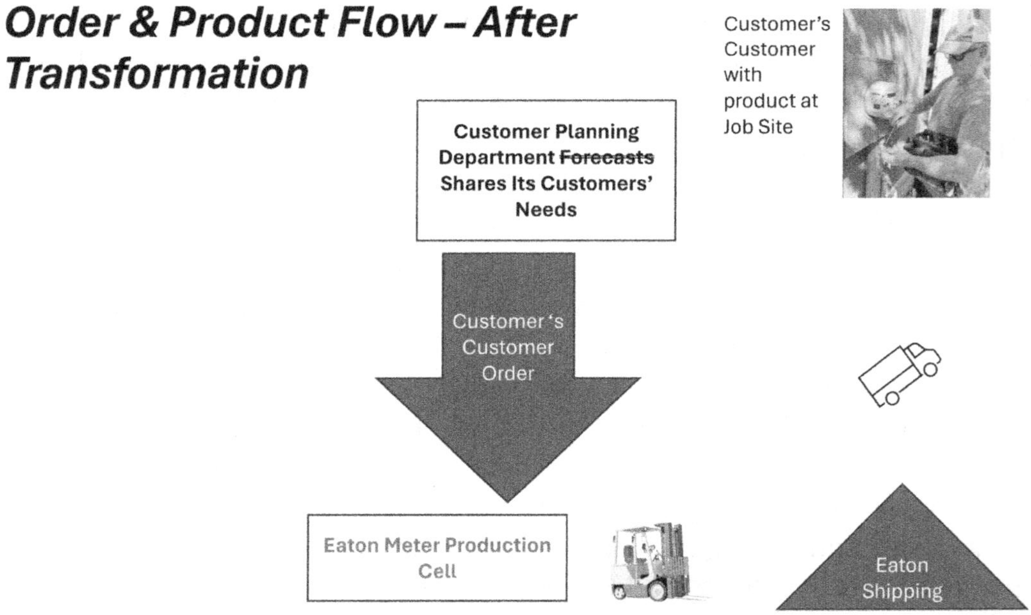

Figure 2.14 Order flow after transformation.

Here is one of the most exciting transformations. We proposed and succeeded in convincing the client that Eaton would manufacture the products and ship within 3 days directly to its customer instead of its finished goods warehouse. This focused factory for metering products no longer would have to guess what the customer would want months in advance, make it, then sit on the products labeled so only the client could sell while we were expediting making what the customer discovered its customers wanted. Not only did the customer agree with this transformation, but they too were also transformed. The customer eliminated all finished goods inventory in its own warehouses, saving them nearly $1,000,000 in finished goods inventory, which again was often not the inventory it needed.

Best of all, Eaton and this major competitor/customer gained a competitive advantage in improved customer service to the electricians. This relationship continues today nearly thirty years later.

Transforming Taking Inventory

Kelly said if you can't complete an inventory in 1 day, "I will find someone who could," Al said. Taking physical inventory was required for financial reporting and compliance in a publicly held corporation. With the old way of moving materials and transacting them and then adjusting inventory manually, inventory counts were often thousands of dollars incorrect. Taking inventory was a horrendous waste of workforce, too. Back in the 1980s, keypunching the inventory counts so the final inventory report could be run was on the critical path to completing the waste of a physical inventory. The backflushing mentioned earlier reduced the number of manual transactions and thus improved the results of the physical inventory caused by human error making so many inventory transactions. But we still had significant inventory count errors that the physical inventory found and corrected. So, Al and his team transformed how we did the physical inventory.

Al put keypunchers on right away. On the day of the inventory, we often waited hours for people to key in the counts. Then, we would have to go out and recount when the first counts showed significant differences. We ran results within the day in descending dollar value gain or loss. Thank goodness we had eliminated a lot of inventory so we had a lot less to count after transforming the factory and having kanban reduce the different locations we had to count the same part.

The transformation of the product structures and backflush had been structured well and the backflush worked with a code of yes or no. During the physical inventory, the team members could not turn in a ticket of a backflushed part thus making it simpler. The computer would calculate the component inventory using the Bill of Material (BOM) to know the quantity of each part in the sub assembly counted. In reconciling during the inventory, we often found key punch errors and resolved these errors quickly. Al prioritized the issues needing resolved knowing that some issues were irrelevant to the outcome.

Al led what many other plants considered amazing – accomplishing a physical inventory in hours vs. days. He benefitted from the transformed manufacturing, information flow, supplier process, and proving to customers we could ship without the customer holding so much inventory.

Scroll and Replicate Success

Every product and every part took a simpler journey inside the Lincoln Plant during the transformation seeing the success in the Industrial Breaker Focused Factory. The Metercenter Factory had its success using concepts from the Industrial Breaker Factory which made the main breakers for Metercenter Factory and the largest of all factories – the Loadcenter Factory.

The loadcenter assembly department prior to the transformation would wait for the breakers made in the industrial breaker area which had to be stored in the stockroom. There breakers were ordered just like everything else – from a forecast of the loadcenter and parts pulled from the stockroom and the breaker sent to the stockroom only to be later pushed to the loadcenter assembly which hoped all the other parts were sent from the stockroom.

The Industrial Breaker Factory worked with the Metercenter and Loadcenter Factories on the main Industrial Breakers used in many of the Metercenter and Loadcenter products. The transformation resulted in the same shift from stocking parts in the stockroom to a Pull system and delivering it right to where the Metercenter and Loadcenter cells would install them.

Leading the Reporting

Leaders must know the capabilities of systems such as the computer. If you have those tools, then this drives a lot of the changes in reporting – simplification. Al had thought about a shipping transaction being the only transaction and omitting the receiving transaction. One transaction vs. many could adjust inventory. After all, grocery stores have between reordering for a long time based on selling the day before.

Manufacturing must have accurate bills of material – what parts are needed. For the few transactions needed after the transformation the plant must have control over scanning or we might not have the right parts at the right time. Just-In-Time manufacturing requires reliable systems because the hordes of inventory sitting around were no longer there. This was good and the point is that we had to transform the transaction process as well and did.

We made a mistake, which is a lesson in sometimes we moved forward only to find quickly that we needed a better way. The adage, "perfection is the enemy of invention," we experienced.

It took Al and I two tries to simplify and reduce the waste of reporting parts moving and adjusting inventory levels. We did not think about the system's capability to figure out that if you shipped an assembly the computer could figure out using the Bill of Material what parts were consumed and then decrement the part's inventory automatically. This eliminated the need to report all of the parts and subassemblies. Thousands of transactions were eliminated with this "Backflush" system.

Transformations will have blips and mistakes and this was one. As the head of Industrial Engineering at the time, I agreed with Al to backflush component parts based on the final product assembly but we had to manually redo the bills of material so each part was at the component level of the final assembly. Think of it as making a cake. The cake was the final product. To make the cake the chef must beat eggs to make the cake batter. Eggs and flour are components of the batter and the batter is a component of the cake. Let's say it took six eggs and four cups of flour for one cake. The Bill of Material looked like this.

Indented Bill of Material

Bill of Material to Bake a Cake. Indented to show making the batter that then is added to a pan to make the cake.									
Level	Component								
1	Eggs								
1	Flour								
1	Sugar								
Step		Make Cake Batter							
2		Grease for pan to reduce sticking							
Step									

This is called an indented Bill of Material. Each level refers to the steps in assembling the components (batter) and assembling the cake. The indented Bill of Material helps us understand that there are common components to cakes, such as batters that can be used to make many different cakes.

We originally "flattened" the BOMs in our excitement to get moving on the idea of eliminating transactions. We thought the computer needed only one level, so every component that went into the cake was listed at one level – not the way components like making the batter got made.

I asked the engineer to change the informative indented Bill of Material, showing each process step as an indentation, to be one level only for the computer to decrement the inventory of the parts. It looked like this:

Simplified Bill of Material for Backflush Automation

Bill of Material to Bake a Cake: "Flattened" to decrement all ingredients				
Level	Component			
1	Eggs			
1	Flour			
1	Sugar			
1	Make Cake Batter			

1	Grease for pan			
2	Bake Cake			
Step				

This was a lot of work just to reduce transactions. The good news was Al and I engaged with the engineer flattening the bills, and we saw how much work flattening bills was. Principle 5: Engage and Go See firsthand, and it paid off. To give direction to employees and not listen and see how those orders played out with the workforces is cruel.

Al and team found that the computer didn't need a flattened bill because there was already a feature in the computer to backflush one or more levels of the cake assembly components. All three in this cake example or the next level prior to the assembly. It was called a backflush yes or no field. This allowed us to keep the hierarchical BOM yet still flatten it virtually.

Sustainability in Transformations

It is not a transformation if it doesn't sustain. I heard about a lot of JIT transformations from consultants and plants claiming such, and what I found was a transformation in language but often no transformation in outcomes.

Buzzwords abounded in the 1980s in manufacturing. Useful buzzwords like Pull, JIT, Cellular Flow, and many others became common, and conferences had speeches with the buzzwords in the title. My suggestion is to keep focused on the KPIs and use buzzwords only if Principle 1: Develop problem-solving skills training uses a few buzzwords. Otherwise, using buzzwords comes off as "showing off" and can detract from the confidence in leaders who use confusing terms.

Worse, some buzzwords are waste. The one I dislike the most is "Gemba." Gemba, or "Go To Gemba," roughly translates from Japanese to "Go See." If we truly want to reduce waste, why would leaders promote speaking an unknown language rather than a word that is understood by the workforce? I respected the people and language I was in and tried to speak as much as possible in their language when I was sure of my skills. Even when I was in Japan teaching, I taught in English and did not assume our definition of Gemba was correct and avoided some of the Japanese words that I was not sure had the same meaning in context that we interpreted.

Transforming the Residential Breaker Factory

Principle 4: Competitive Force Strategy – "I'll never forget trying to start up C40/3," Al said. C40/3 was the code name for the project to take the cost out of the residential breaker product line. Lincoln leadership prior to Al returning from Asheville was trying to lower the cost of labor to assemble the breakers.

Al came back to Lincoln and learned Lincoln had outsourced some breaker production to a small firm in the Midwest. Lincoln was desperate to lower the cost, and this was one of several ideas.

Automation was eventually the strategy chosen. All of Eaton's competitors had moved residential breaker production to low cost labor countries despite making most of the parts in the USA and shipping them overseas only to ship back the assembled breaker.

The competitive environment demanded observance of Principle 4 – Competitive Force Strategy. Lincoln's transformation included the most significant redesign of the residential line of circuit breakers in years. C40/3 was the name of the program Don Link and his team led in redesigning. The name captured the key transformation goal – cut 40% of the cost within 3 years. To accomplish this, engineering in design had to solve for some of the variability. Eaton's strategy was to automate the manufacturing and assembly process to reduce the cost and to continue as the only major competitor manufacturing in the USA.

All of Eaton's competitors had moved residential breaker production to low cost labor countries despite making most of the parts in the USA and shipping them overseas only to ship back the assembled breaker.

The redesign required major component changes, including "drop-in" assembly required for automation at the time. Assembly required twisting, lifting, and some finesse. Automation needed parts that could be lowered onto each other without the benefit of a worker's finesse.

The strategy was bold because we started with the design of the product to make it easier to manufacture and selectively automated not only final assembly but also manufacturing key components. An example is the bimetal assembly, the core of a residential circuit breaker, which not only had holes punched for assembly screws, but the new process also tapped the hole, eliminating all the handling and extra steps to later tap the needed calibration hole.

Training in Product Design and Design of Process Problem-Solving

Problem-solving training is not just training frontline employees in PDCA or Six Sigma or other methods focused on change management, productivity, or waste. Think of how every business begins – it begins with a product or service design. What happens to a start-up business if the design and the process of making or delivering the design fail with customers? Capability is first and foremost the measure of a business. A successful product is a product that is able, that is, capable of meeting a customer's want.

Don Link and his team of engineers were responsible for product designs manufactured in Lincoln. A design engineer's role included training manufacturing on how to make the products. Post initial production, Lincoln's engineers and Don's team worked together problem-solving for the inevitable variability of complex products like circuit breakers, which have many parts with tight tolerances requiring low variability.

Variability can come from the raw materials supplied to Lincoln, plastic parts made in Lincoln, and many of the multiple steps taken in welding, assembling, and even testing which every circuit breaker had to pass. A good design is robust to the inevitable variation, and we were trained to reduce those variation problems.

The challenge with automation was that variability caused component variability. Our workers were adept at assembly when the parts didn't quite fit together and they could adjust for component variation. The human could also see a plastic part that had a visual defect and scrap it. Also necessary was in the testing of the breaker. The person operating the tester routinely recalibrated the breaker to trip the breaker at the right time when an overload occurred.

Al knew Lincoln was struggling when he asked how many breakers were produced by the new automation. He heard 3. Al said, 3,000? No, three breakers. Automated assembly was, well let us say, a discovery of over-automation. John Deere concluded years before us that a "Lights Out" factory is the ultimate. Lights out meaning no human was needed who needed to see in the factory. John Deere eventually found at time it over automated and reverted back to manual assembly. It found some complex operations were difficult to be automated.

Eaton Purchases Its Competitor – Westinghouse

Transformations do not happen in a vacuum and this story is another success from the transformation.

Eaton purchased its competitor which was about three times bigger in volume than Lincoln-produced product lines. Lincoln's transformation helped it survive this major acquisition around 1995.

Westinghouse's similar power distribution division was three times the size of the Eaton business unit. Westinghouse was also the market leader in the industrial breaker products.

Westinghouse made many of the same products in multiple plants that Lincoln made. Residential and Industrial Breakers, Metercenters, and Loadcenters.

The acquisition was an opportunity to reduce capacity in the industry and improve profitability for Eaton.

Success and Survival – Thanks to the Transformation

The Lincoln Plant competed with Westinghouse plants to be the manufacturing site for the same product lines. Eaton Lincoln won the competition because of its transformation and leadership team and now was the sole manufacturing site for loadcenters and metering devices despite Westinghouse's much larger facilities in the US. Absorbing loadcenters and metering required Lincoln to absorb 3X its volume. The transformation made this possible. Special recognition is owed to Ken Billinger, Marketing Leader, and his team for literally living with the Lincoln team for months to direct all the incoming new orders. The new focused factory organizational structure and reporting system supported Ken, Sheri, and his onsite team in getting Lincoln making the right products at the right time. However, we had to give up being the circuit breaker site because the products we won would consume much more space in Lincoln. Thus, Westinghouse plants became the manufacturing site for residential breakers.

A different outcome for the industrial breaker line was a result of government regulation. The US Government only allowed Eaton to purchase Westinghouse if it sold the Industrial Breaker line because Westinghouse was the US market leader in the line and the regulatory agencies feared Eaton would gain monopolistic powers.

Thus, Lincoln's first Focused Factory production equipment was sold to Thomas and Betts. Lincoln received a big compliment from Thomas and

Betts when it decided to manufacture the same way as Lincoln – the transformed Lincoln

Eaton started the consolidation of operations including manufacturing to capitalize on the synergy from the sale. We moved the huge and many assets needed to manufacture the Westinghouse products into Lincoln. The transformed processes, organization, reporting, and mindset transformed how every Westinghouse product was made and shipped.

Designing with Manufacturing – Simultaneously

The transformation starting in 1980s included a much bigger contribution to design in the Metering Focused Factory including Jim Campbell's success in leading a significant reduction in electrical connections within the complex metering devices. Every electrical connection is an opportunity to fail and may result in excessive heat build-up and fire. Jim and the team of manufacturing engineers and in-house automation builders teamed with Milwaukee design engineering in eliminating connections by redesigning the bus bar system inside each metering device. This effort also improved reliability by eliminating parts and making assembly easier.

Power Outlet Panel Birth – Design and Manufacturing Story

The power outlet panel was a product line born in Lincoln. The original idea was to provide temporary power in the music industry. I was a manager at Lincoln and a drummer in a cover band. My band needed more power than what most stages provided due to our light show and thus we had to connect directly to the venue's loadcenter or panelboard. Lincoln made everything needed in a panel often called a "temporary power panel" except the receptacles which we ended up buying. Eaton had never provided a product for what the industry calls a temporary power panel, convention center panel, RV power panel, and various other twists. Lincoln shared the ROI justification to allow Lincoln to develop a product line with division design engineering and the product line launched under budget and on time. This was a Six Sigma Lean designed product line from the start and capitalized on the transformed order receipt to product shipment processes. The assembly cell included for the first time a stamping press that allowed any item – any day shipment from hundreds of configuration potentials. The customer could choose from hundreds of receptacle combinations thus requiring different covers from which the receptacles would protrude from the inner cover. The assembly cell had everything it needed including the same direct-to-cell order receipt system Lincoln pioneered in its metering production.

Lincoln Today

I visited Lincoln in 2024 and bumped into the plant's Supply Chain Leader. He confirmed the program in metering continues 25 years later. I know the leadership and employees have made significant improvements to what we transformed in the mid-1980s through the mid-1990s when I took a position at the Group level. I am certain the transformation was a big reason I was selected for this role. It sure wasn't because of my singing ability.

Sustaining Transformations

Eaton Lincoln wins the 2010 Assembly Plant of the Year: Lean Thinking Helps Eaton Stay Healthy.[5] Well after Al and I left, Lincoln continued to excel. Assembly Magazine awarded Lincoln, Eaton's loadcenter, metering devices, power outlet panels, air conditioner disconnects, and generator transfer switches assembly plant its 7th annual award. High reliability continues at Lincoln maintaining the processes developed initially in the late 1980s and 1990s as it transformed from a functionally organized manufacturing layout to a continuous flow product and customer organized facility. Boston Consulting Group (BCG) joins Assembly Magazine in researching the best assembly plants. Mike Zinser, partner and managing director in BCG's Chicago office and a co-leader of its global manufacturing process at the time of the award supported Lincoln's award. He shared, "Eaton's Lincoln facility stood out based on its strong overall performance and its ability to continuously improve..." He adds about reliability, "Many organizations claim to have lean programs, but they often fail to sustain their improvements over long periods of time. This isn't the case at Eaton. The production system and lean thinking have become an embedded part of the culture where employees constantly strive for competitive advantage in their operations." The article continues that Lincoln has designed or assisted in the design of products.

Summary

Th Eaton stories of its transformations included reaching a level of excellence never achieved before. All eight principles are in evidence then and still today. Leaders who know the principles and apply them in any order increase the probability of achieving performance/outcomes that often provide a competitive advantage, like Eaton enjoys. The pandemic beginning around 2021 provides further proof of sustaining the competitive advantage planned and gained from efforts of the design, manufacturing, and distribution teams who transformed Lincoln operations during the transformation back in the 1980s. Lincoln was swamped with loadcenter orders during the pandemic. Its chief competitor had only offshore production and its plants were shut down for extended periods.

The Eaton Lincoln transformation is a story that can help most manufacturers and the details in this chapter hopefully is relevant and helpful for all manufacturers.

Al and I presented this transformation at conferences whose attendees often were looking for solutions to improve productivity, operations, quality, financial returns, and other KPIs. This interest remains today and may be because the root causes still exist such as losing ground to competitors, overly complex systems, poor quality, workforce discontent, and government regulation that is dysfunctional and may cause more harm. Healthcare consultants often come from manufacturing and the same principles work in healthcare as we will see in our healthcare transformation chapter.

Attendees have asked what the spark was to start. Some wanted to know how middle management supported or resisted the changes. Eaton's catalyst was competitive cost pressure. Middle management stepped up and supervisors like Marc and Chuck brought the vision to reality and they were joined by peers across the facility. The frontline employees were instrumental in redesigning, transforming, how flow could be achieved, replacing the batch manufacturing common in many manufacturing facilities.

What does Eaton's transformation not cover? Eaton did not have to contend as much as other industries government regulatory restrictions and pressures. We'll address this pressure with facts and observations on government's contribution to problems in the healthcare transformation and financial services transformation stories.

Tips for Manufacturing, Information, Distribution, Organizing, and Layout Transformations

Al and I list tips for leaders to achieve excellence. We include things we would have done differently. Hopefully, these save readers from making the same mistakes. These tips should be helpful for any industry and organization producing a routine service or manufacturing. I deployed elements in multiple manufacturing sites and healthcare, especially in surgical services and emergency departments where patient flow is critical to quality and satisfaction.

- Automation (or not). Ask if you can move the production easily and avoid automation that might be considered because of obstacles creating waste such as parts moving excessively. The automation vendor hired to achieve 100% automation of the circuit breaker failed us in many ways. We never achieved the capability in production quantity expected. We learned to not over automate.
- Queuing products/components for production – The over-automation resulted in key parts not arriving on time for assembly. An engineer and I used simulation/animation proving that a small buffer of these components would increase production when the component flow was struggling due to machine breakdown or quality issues. The lesson learned is to stay with the solution until proven. The engineer handed the information off to the floor engineer for a queuing conveyor. A queuing conveyor allows parts to accumulate and then dispenses immediately if the production line needs a part. Unfortunately, the floor engineer paid thousands of dollars for a fixed conveyor, not the queuing conveyor we recommended. A fixed conveyor is like the conveyor belt at a sushi restaurant. Once a customer before you takes a dish, that slot on the conveyor stays empty (and you starve).
- The lesson is to understand variation and then work to eliminate it. When elimination of the root cause is impossible, then create a robust solution. A robust solution is one that succeeds despite variation.
- Be realistic on cost saving potential. A large redesign was to cut 40% of the costs in 3 years. This did not happen because of the over-automation. Before we started, the engineering people thought that total automation was a dumb idea but leadership pushed ahead. We should have

worked harder on Principle 5: Engage-Go See. John Deere and other companies experienced over-automation.

- We discussed bills of material and the indentation shows some of the complexity of many steps to make a product. The transformation included a complete change in the way breakers were tested for their primary function – interrupting electrical flow when a fault occurs. This testing is done on every breaker to ensure safety. All breakers were assembled and then moved to test stations where other employees picked up the breaker again and tested it. When the test failed, the person who assembled the breaker received no feedback and thus had no ability to calibrate to improve the test successes. An engineer designed small test stations for each assembly station. This assembler now placed the breaker into the tester and was able to assemble the next breaker while the tester tested the prior one. The assembler now got immediate feedback and could help calibrate for a successful test and help root cause analysis when test failed. We strived for robust manufacturing for when we could not design-out variation.
- Improving what is measured. Al and I redefined how to measure production. As the head of industrial engineering, our engineers spent most of their day measuring how much product should be made per time unit. The individual incentive system required this "standard" to know how much incentive pay was earned. The department had a KPI which was the sum of all of the individual production transactions. The middle management was reinforced using this KPI. Al and I knew that there were a lot more resources deployed than using just the work eligible for production. Perhaps this was 60% of the total hours of all human resources? Missing were all of the support staff to move materials, to check quality, all of the stockroom employees, the maintenance staff, and tool makers were all missing in this KPI for productivity. Worse, the individual incentive system reinforced producing regardless of quality.

  Al got us the data so we could measure all of the resources and we created a team productivity measure. Now we had a baseline to know how the transformation was impacting all of the work being done (Labor costs compared to product costs shipped).
- Principle 3: SMART with Radical Goals – Improve Profitability. The big KPI, making no mistake about it, is profitability for Eaton. The manufacturing plant is measured on what it most controls – cost. Our job plain and simple was to manage costs and labor productivity was a major

factor. A year after the transformation, productivity was still breaking records.

- Work and roles change – I realigned industrial engineering to focus on improving processes more now that the individual incentive system measurement was not as important as total work. The more macro focus of all labor was comprehensive to include all labor and much easier to measure than recording what each individual did. There was not one role that was not impacted by the transformation of which I can think. Al and I went to see some of the employees who earned the most extra money in the old individual incentive program expecting significant pushback. We did not find that. In fact, one of the women who earned the most was relieved getting a flat 25% or so increase and not having the stress every hour of every day in having the parts to earn the incentive.
- Cellular flow vs. Batch manufacturing: In the Industrial Breaker factory, switching to cellular flow was the biggest contributor to productivity improvement. The breakers were very effective in the six person "U" shaped cell. Before each operator assembled at a station only to put finished assemblies into a pan and then shipped to the stockroom and days or longer later moved back to a station often not far from the prior station.
- Quality improved: The quality output was significantly improved in the industrial breaker by having the six employees in the U shaped cell give immediate feedback to each other and problem-solve when a failure arose. We mentioned the tester process earlier and there were more transformative process changes throughout the plant thanks to the frontline and service employees.
- Good incentives are key. We gave everyone a pay increase, which was approximately what the total payout with incentive. Even fork truck drivers earned more who never had a chance to earn incentive pay but could help or hinder others making incentive in how well they brought parts to those earning incentive.
- Al adds, "a lot of people seem to want to control information. It is foolish. What can a leader do that a person on the floor cannot do? There is not much you can do but gripe about it." Al and I stressed showing the people data and reality as Chuck and Marc did and let them help. Team members worked for the team goal.
- WSJ article (Late 1980s). Sandy Cutler and his counterpart leading Eaton Automotive, George Dettloff, chose Lincoln and Kearney Nebraska

when asked by the Wall Street Journal to show them Eaton's most successful plants.

- Pete Krol, the GM at Headquarters, was very supportive.
- Transforming the Organization – Focused Factories highlighted a lot of support jobs that weren't really necessary. Once the one stock location was achieved, we did not need so much material handling. We reassigned many employees to more productive work.
- Designed products post Transformation – The RV/Convention Center product line was the first product designed with the transformed Lincoln production process in mind. Sarah Cook was the Industrial Engineer assigned to the design. She designed the same U Cell concept as in the Industrial Breaker Focused Factory. The Power Panel Cell could make any product any day and ship direct order and to stock. She even had the punch press at the assembly cell to stamp the inner cover to house thousands of combinations of receptacles.

Notes

1. Found at Key Bank https://www.key.com/about/company-information/leadership/cutler-bio.html
2. For more Information: https://educationlibrary.org/theory-x-and-theory-y-douglas-mcgregor/
3. More at https://www.investors.com/news/dockworkers-strike-pay-hike-cripple-economy-union-leader-tru/
4. Found at https://www.isc.hbs.edu/strategy/business-strategy/Pages/the-five-forces.aspx
5. Found at https://www.assemblymag.com/articles/88251-customers-always-come-first-at-eaton-lincoln

Chapter 3

Transforming an Organization

Organizations may have just completed a strategic plan that changes the direction significantly. Measured as we would a transformation, the strategic plan outcomes will often be a transformation in performance. Now is the time to ensure their organizational structure is best to achieve the strategy. For some, this may require a transformation of their organizational structure and thus the reason for this chapter.

Structure follows strategy – not precedes it.

In 2022, Elon Musk purchased Twitter, now named X. In its latest Annual Report,[1] X discusses its organizational structure and strategy for growth.

The report states, "We depend on highly skilled personnel to grow and operate our business. If we are unable to hire, retain, and motivate our personnel, we may not be able to grow effectively."

X is a social media giant that firmly believes in utilizing the 3Ms, as noted throughout its report of risks and impacts to its Key Performance Indicator (KPI), Monetizable Daily Active Usage or Users (MDAU).

Transformations through Applying the Principles – Not Reorganizing

Creating or having a transformation department or another organization named with transformation in the name is often not correlated with achieving transforming performance. Why? Chandler[2] believes that structure should follow strategy. I consider groups of people transformation experts, but only after radical change has occurred. Being named a transformation

 DOI: 10.4324/9781032639574-3

organization is a badge of honor earned after an achievement. Professions earn the title just like one is not a lawyer until one has passed the bar. If your company has a transformation group, ask for the evidence that earned the name. If they have led radical change, congratulate them. If they have not as an organization, I would never use the word to describe the organization. It is almost a curse to achieve, I think, because I recall only one transformation success from an organization named a transformation group. I cover this in the Healthcare chapter.

Naming a new organization a transformation group is failing to recognize that structure follows strategy. Consultants may use the term loosely, suggesting they can help an organization achieve transformative outcomes. I know firsthand that some major companies have recruited a new transformation group in the hope that this group will result in transformative outcomes. I have worked in a couple "Transformation" organizations with only one earning the title.

Eaton's transformations were led by line managers, including myself. My second career at *Svenska Kullagerfabriken* (translated to Swedish Ball Bearing Factory most commonly known as SKF) transformed its Quality organization in the Seals Division USA and was done without a department with the word transformation in its name. We simply did it under our department named the US Quality Group. I am not suggesting there have not been transformations elsewhere in the world led by a department that calls itself a transformation organization. My coaching to readers is to save the energy in putting transformation in the name and spend time more wisely following the principles and supporting teammates who can solve problems. Don't think that the people grouped to achieve transformative change need an organization named transformation to achieve transformations. Instead, promote the heroes and support them in line roles to achieve excellence and transformation in outcomes.

I have found that the executive in charge of an organization, which was named a transformation department, actually slowed progress. Why? Because in one instance, the leader was not applying the principles of measurement (Principles 2, and 3) and training the workforce in problem-solving (Principle 1). He was fuzzy on the strategy (Principle 4) and never went through the process to observe and interact to understand reality (Principle 5). There may have been no measures prioritized nor tested for truth. Maybe not surprising is to find leaders in transformation organizations who have titles of Six Sigma Black Belt or Master Black Belt who profess never achieving the requirements which include project successes. Without the rigor of success, claiming the title of transformation or Belt level is puffery. Maybe we should apply Six Sigma's Measurement System Analysis for assessing titles, too. Better yet, and this is my point, start applying the principles and get the transformative outcomes. Avoid the titles.

The beauty of the principles is that the order of applying is not critical. The leadership sponsoring a transformation organization to deliver transformative outcomes should lead with Principle 4: Competitive force strategy and then look if the organizational structure is matched to achieve. Start also with Principle 2: Utilize the 3Ms, and Principle 3: Help the organization create SMART radical goals.

I would invest in a good Master Black Belt (MBB). She is taught how to lead leaders in developing strategies and is also skilled in solving problems. As Mike Fenger, the former Chief Quality Officer (CQO) of Motorola, taught Motorola's Executive Vice Presidents (VPs), invite your MBB to your strategy session as you would your Finance and Human Resources (HR) teammates. The MBB will help distil strategy and support it with measures of outcome. Your MBB may be more in tune with the issues and will help identify where transformations are most beneficial. She will then shift to supporting those leading the transformation through the entire problem-solving effort and setting up sustainment with statistical control.

Principle 4: Structure Follows Strategy

Transformations are measured by outcomes – not by who is in what role. Several times in my career, the CEO announced an organizational change to transform the company. Never did the reorganization result in better outcomes. In one well-known corporation, which is now a shell of its former self, the reorganization preceded the breaking up of the corporation. What was once a market share leading company in three different industries is now a market leader in only one. I reported to the CQO and I was concerned if the corporation was going to exit the automotive business. He replied that its strategy required a presence in automotive to capture synergy with its other businesses in communications and so no sale.

Months later, the corporation sold its automotive business and was on the path to losing its market share leadership in its consumer communications market. An organization supposedly created for a strategy to grow was reorganized and correlated with market share losses. Maybe reorganizing the structure before the strategy resulted in a failed strategy? It seems the end result was a major reorganization (selling off businesses) that resulted from a lack of capability over time – reliability.

Worse is when the organization restructures around a faulty strategy. Several times, I was in a corporation that was struggling in some businesses, and they would call for a reorganization. The results were not any better. So, either the reorganization did not match the strategy because results were still below expectations, or the strategy was weak.

Regardless, the energy and disruption of reorganizing might have been better spent following the principles within the existing structure. After a transformation, strategy is always clearer, and then restructuring, such as at the Eaton Lincoln Plant, supports more improvement and sustainment of outcomes.

A.D. Chandler's work in 1962 resulted in suggesting that an organizational structure should be designed to meet strategy which was exactly the sequence that Eaton Corporation took in the Lincoln plant transformations.

Chandler studied companies from the 1850s to the 1920s, including DuPont, General Motors, and Sears Roebuck. "Structure follows strategy" is a business principle coined by Chandler. He states that the organizational structure of a business (the divisions, departments, teams, processes, technology, etc.) is best designed to achieve a firm's strategy. Chandler found that to achieve a strategy, one should ensure that the organizational structure supports the strategy. I add that one should lead with the strategy and then support the organization in applying the principles.

Chandler concluded,

> market-driven proliferation of product lines led to a shift from a functional, monolithic organizational form to a more loosely coupled divisional structure. Having developed the best possible strategy, companies could then determine the most appropriate organizational structure to achieve it.

The Eaton Lincoln Plant's story supports rearranging organizations after transforming outcomes is possible if not already proven.

Strategy comes first, with structure organized to achieve the strategy, and structure then feeds the culture spread and sustainment. My experience in transformations is a bit different across companies considering the culture spread. We always considered the culture in developing the organizational structure rather than the structure dictating the culture. At Eaton, our culture was very much participative, even with the collective bargaining unit. To fight that culture, to become more directive and dictatorial, I think we would have failed to achieve the goals and outcomes. Another company had a very hierarchical command and control structure and we included organizational changes to allow and reinforce more participation.

In organizations that failed to achieve radical improvements, I found the culture did not match the organizational structure. An example is a services firm I was consulting with, which was very dedicated to serving its members but had a functional hierarchical structure that inhibited frontline team members and managers from solving problems. The formal structure restricted them from achieving the strategy of "Customer first" because it missed the flexibility at the frontline to solve customer issues. Its KPI of customer loyalty continued to lose ground to competitors. I wondered what they could have achieved with a more customer-oriented organizational structure, perhaps with people organized by customer group and the entire product life cycle represented on the same team vs. the functionally aligned organizational structure it had. When I asked my consulting staff to convene a meeting of those who sold products with those who serviced the customers, it was clear the structure did not meet the strategy because the two teams said it was their first time meeting together.

Leading to Excel: Martin Swarbrick

Martin Swarbrick is an experienced Chief Executive Officer, Strategic Advisor, and Corporate Director who has led large global organizations and mid-sized private companies in high technology, engineering, and manufacturing in the U.S. and Europe. His strategic acumen and deep grounding in the disciplines of the Malcolm Baldrige National Quality Award have enabled him to successfully transform business models, operating processes, and organizational structures that increase stakeholder value in periods of stagnation, growth, and market upheaval.

Following his graduation from Trinity College in Dublin, Ireland, with degrees in Engineering and Mathematics, Martin began his career with GE. Kodak then recruited him to lead its Verbatim operations in Europe, a global technology company that produced highly engineered products for Microsoft and other market leaders. He joined Motorola's Commercial, Government, and Industrial Solutions Sector (CGISS and now Motorola Solutions) and became VP and General Manager of a Greenfield operation in Dublin, Ireland, that grew quickly under his leadership.

Motorola transferred Martin to the USA as VP of Business Excellence where he led the implementation of a rigorous global operations framework based on the Baldrige criteria that impacted 14K employees in 21 facilities and businesses serving 27 million users in 170 countries around the world. Motorola was recognized with the Malcolm Baldridge for Performance Excellence in 2002. Based upon his successful track record, he was recruited to Bison Gear and Engineering Corporation, a private family engineering and manufacturing company, where he served as president and CEO for nine years.

Martin was VP of Business Excellence for Motorola's CGISS when I joined Motorola. Martin led the team that was recognized when Motorola won the Malcolm Baldrige Award for Performance Excellence in 2002, Motorola's second win. He was a member of Robert (Bob) L. Barnett's senior leadership team. Bob was the executive leading Motorola's CGISS. *Industry Week* reported that Motorola, "Among other practices, CGISS uses 'Performance Excellence Scorecards' in the implementation of strategic objectives and employs 'M-Gates,' an integrated product-development and life-cycle process administered by cross-functional product teams." An *Industry Week* article[3] adds, "We are enormously pleased and honored by this recognition of our business-wide, continuous-improvement process," says Robert L. Barnett, executive VP of Motorola Inc., and president and CEO of CGISS.

Martin's experiences support the principles of transformations. Martin and I cover Motorola winning Baldrige the second time under Martin's leadership. We also share his work today advising business owners and next-generation leaders on how to transform their organizations to create more value.

Winning Baldrige once is an amazing achievement, and winning it twice is phenomenal. The recognition that Motorola's first transformation resulted in the first-ever Malcolm Baldrige Award had a lasting impact. Having co-led Eaton Lincoln's first preparation for assessment against the Baldrige criteria, I can attest that it is a full-time job on top of your existing role. The Baldrige criteria had changed from the award in 1988 which was for all of Motorola. The focus then was on the quality of the product as it came out of production. Six Sigma, which was started by Motorola, was well underway. As Martin explained, today the Baldrige criteria are focused on business Performance Excellence.

Martin points out that one of the keys to organizational transformation is to have a leader with a vision and passion for excellence and continuous improvement. Bob was that leader. The culture of Total Customer Satisfaction (TCS) and project/program management that already existed throughout CGISS were key factors in enabling the work required to drive a renewed effort for a step function change in continuous improvement. Martin explained,

> with a clear business imperative to accelerate performance, a team culture, a committed leadership team, and a proven Baldrige framework for Performance Excellence, the die was cast. Getting everyone aligned with the prioritized opportunities for improvement in each of the seven categories enabled us to address one of the challenges in change management and transformation in any business, addressing the white spaces.

White spaces are the gaps in understanding interactions, challenges, and opportunities for improvements between functions.

An example using Martin's point is found in Eaton. We focused on the handoff from design engineering to manufacturing engineering to ensure a minimum of "White space." A design may look perfect on paper to the designer, only to find that there is no way to manufacture it in the plant. At Eaton, in the Power Outlet Panel development I led, we ensured manufacturing engineering and design engineering had regular and frequent handoffs. We continually tested concepts and eventually how well the design fit with the manufacturing equipment and personnel to ensure manufacturability. This practice of ensuring a design is manufacturable has been labelled "Design for Manufacturing," but this is inappropriate. We design for the customer, and designing something for manufacturability is a given.

Martin reported to Greg Brown after Robert Barnett retired from Motorola, and Greg became the Chairman and Chief Executive Officer of the renamed Motorola Solutions. Greg has led Motorola Solutions, which has been named one of the World's Best Companies by *Time* magazine, listed among *Newsweek*'s Most Trustworthy Companies, and considered one of the World's Most Innovative Companies by Fast Company. Greg was named one of the top CEOs in America by Barron's in 2023.

Martin was forever open to discussions on quality and business excellence, and I learned much from him and his team about high reliability. I remember one of his stories about firefighter radios. Motorola had some failures in the field with radios used by wildfire crews not turning on or off. Principle 5: Engage and Go See helped solve the problem. Engineers went out to the wildfire area and found that firefighters had very large gloves and they found it difficult to depress the button with those huge gloves on. In trying to turn their radios on or off, the gloves made it difficult to push the radio's on/off switch, so it was widespread practice to bang the radio switch against tree bark to depress the button. Seeing the firefighters struggling firsthand, the engineers redesigned the switch to better accommodate gloved hands.

Martin and the other senior leaders reporting to Bob worked as champions with the seven cross-functional global teams tasked to lead the strategy to win Baldrige the second time. The senior leaders each had one of the seven categories of the Baldrige framework to champion. Bob himself led the leadership category. With that level of engagement and support for their respective teams, the 4-year journey to drive the opportunities to improve Performance Excellence began. After making considerable progress, the team felt it was time to validate the improvements.

The decision was made to apply for the Performance Excellence award. What better way to verify the transformations than to have an outside team of very senior professional businesspeople from other industries, trained as Baldrige examiners, come into the organization and engage, observe, and report the findings to the organization. Martin adds, "It gave the organization the opportunity to show proudly what had been achieved but at the same time emphasized that continuous improvement is a never-ending journey, as the visit report verifies achievements and lists further opportunities for improvement."

The following list of highlights exemplifies Motorola's achievements and supports our definition of excellence and transformation. Note the highlighting of excellence and transformation as the National Institute of Standards and Technology (NIST) describes the Malcolm Baldrige Award. It would do any organization well, I think, to learn and apply against the criteria that Motorola and other winners of this prestigious award were measured against to win. The NIST shares on its website information about the Malcolm Baldrige Award on Motorola winning the award in 2002:

Highlights of Motorola's Achievements:

- Employee productivity, measured as sales per employee, increased 32% over the 1999–2002 period.
- Over the past 3 years, overall customer satisfaction and repurchase/recommend satisfaction levels have exceeded 88%.
- Since 1999, CGISS has had a 7% return on assets versus a negative average for the telecommunications industry.

- CGISS recycled 57% of its non-hazardous waste and has reduced emissions by 88% since 1996.

To appreciate what CGISS accomplished, I share the following from the National Baldrige group from its NIST under the USA Department of Commerce's website[4].

Did you know?

Organizations are using Baldrige to gain a competitive edge over their competition.

What makes Baldrige different?

Baldrige helps organizations address a dynamic environment, focus on strategy-driven performance, achieve customer and workforce engagement, and improve governance and ethics, societal responsibilities, competitiveness, and long-term organizational sustainability. It offers a comprehensive management approach that focuses on results in all areas, organizational and personal learning, and knowledge sharing.

What Is Performance Excellence?

The term "Performance Excellence®" refers to an integrated approach to organizational performance management that results in

- Delivery of increasing value to customers and stakeholders, contributing to organizational sustainability.
- Improvement of overall organizational effectiveness and capabilities
- Organizational and personal learning.

Baldrige Excellence Framework

The Baldrige Excellence Framework® is the Baldrige Program's signature product. The Baldrige framework booklet includes the Criteria for Performance Excellence®, a set of questions that represent the leading edge of validated leadership and management practice. Through the Baldrige framework and Criteria, the Baldrige Program provides global leadership in promoting Performance Excellence and the learning and sharing of successful performance practices, principles, and strategies.

Twenty years later Motorola Solutions is still the market leader and the choice of radios in my county's Emergency Services District. I was a commissioner for the County Fire Commission and was proud to see these First Responders all using Motorola radios. The only complaint I ever heard from the Fire Chief about the radios was related to needing to shift to the latest model. The current radios are still working very well, but like most electronic devices, innovations are highly valued, and a company eventually decides to stop supporting older models. I learned firsthand while at Eaton that semiconductor chips are often the limiting factor in how long a device can be repaired. The semiconductor industry's nature is to shift product equipment over to making new chips and eliminating the ability to continue to manufacture outdated chips. First Responder radios are no exception. Motorola's reliability continues thanks to its Six Sigma and original transformation practices when Motorola earned its first, and the nation's first, Malcolm Baldrige Award. That is sustainment.

Martin's Executive Consulting and Advisory Work

Martin at the time of this book is a senior partner with ProLink Investment Inc., a principal with the Brentwood Advisory Group, and the Founder and CEO of Clear Waters LLC, a Chicago-based firm, which advises and coaches private business owners and next-generation leaders and executives focused on generating increased value by ensuring their organizations are ready and attractive to transition under their control and timeline. He is an expert in governance, operations, and strategy for private mid-market companies.

His experience includes serving on manufacturing, association, and software/technology boards and has had ownership in manufacturing and service companies in the US and Europe. He is a credentialed Certified Exit Planning Advisor (CEPA) and is an alumnus of the Leading Family Enterprises and Corporate Governance programs at Northwestern's Kellogg School of Business.

Martin practiced Principle 1: Problem-Solving Skill Development by constantly gaining new skills and tools. He recently received his Certified Exit Planning Advisor credentials. He is using these well-proven skills from his time at Motorola to advise executives, next-generation leaders, and business owners to accelerate value in their businesses.

I asked Martin for his definition of transformation. "We start with the end game in mind, but we constantly revisit that every 90 days." He shared that in the case of private business owners; a transformation begins with discovering the personal and financial readiness of the owner and an assessment of what the business attractiveness might look like to an outside third party. The next step is to create a detailed roadmap. In many cases, transformations require a significant change in business and/or operating models to ensure alignment. One of the challenges is to educate and ensure the leaders understand that the transition from "as is" to "what will be" will take time and stamina. They will need to embrace change and be ready for resistance. Transformations require time and stamina. Change is not easy.

Martin shares that a simple exercise is to ask them to try to change some habits a leader has. For example, in the case of one client, it was obvious that he was overworking, including working weekends, and not even taking lunch breaks. The task given to the individual was to leave the facility each day over the next 2 weeks and take a 45-minute lunch break for a minimum of 3 days/week with no email or phone calls. The client had to record each day what happened. It turned out to be a difficult change to make, and it took much longer to get to 3 days. That was a small change! It takes a lot of perseverance to make a large transformative change. It also takes backbone and heart to move an organization. Martin shared, "Getting this balance right can be a challenge for many when things get tough." Martin shared one other story.

> I remember when I was VP and General Manager, Motorola's Radio Product Operations, Land Mobile Products Sector. I was leading the startup of a new facility in Dublin, Ireland. We grew to over 1,700 people in 5 years in a brand-new purpose-built facility. One of the many challenges we faced was engaging all our people in problem-solving in the areas they had the control to make change. We put everyone through a problem-solving course and then assigned them to small teams. At one time we had between 70% and 80% of the total population on teams. The steering team came to me one day and said that the teams seemed to be struggling to get time consistently to work on their projects. I decided that we would shut down for an hour each week to work on their problem-solving projects. This included all functions. As a result, I was amazed at the innovative ideas, solutions, and the reduction in time to resolve problems that came from these Total Customer Satisfaction (TCS) teams. When I challenged the steering team to figure out how we could get everyone to have the opportunity to

see the work of each of the teams, they created a flip chart-sized template that each team could fill in. They then posted all the completed projects around the large facilities walls. I watched and saw the people reading these charts at various breaks or on their way in or out of work. I was able to see learning firsthand. But I learned something else during that opportunity. There is much value in working alongside an amazingly talented team of people. As an individual, we must constantly renew our skills. Keep doing the right things right, while addressing often what needs to be changed. Don't fear starting again. As a leader, be capable of being replaced. But be ready to take on the challenge to transform or start again.

Jennifer Tice on Transformations and Leadership in Financial Services

Jennifer Tice, Ph.D., is an accomplished Human Resources executive who specializes in transforming and building organizations. Jennifer started her career in consulting and has focused her work on achieving transformations. Her experience combines strong soft skills with data analytics skills. She consults through close, strategic partnerships with the business. Her philosophy centers on the integration of people, processes, and technology to drive successful outcomes, with a strong foundation in data analytics, collaborative processes, and innovative technology. Her firm's consulting work has consistently delivered valuable results for her clients.

When asked to define transformation, Jennifer thinks it is going from one state, from point A and doing a pivot to point B. Transformation is a shift. A transformation must be recognizable by others – others must sense the shift. A transformation is something one can see, hear, or feel. In culinary transformations, maybe even taste and smell something have changed remarkably.

Transformation can also occur within a person. Jennifer was coaching a woman who had lost her confidence. After coaching her on what she wanted and how to express her ideas, she changed how she approached decisions and others around her. Jennifer's client shared after Jennifer's coaching that her health was better and she was sleeping better. Jennifer found that her client “transformed from a victim to a person with true agency,”. Her client transformed into a person who could direct her own life and determine her own outcomes. Jennifer taught her that, “one can let things happen, or have agency over life.”

Jennifer remembers some clients thinking they had a transformation but failed. Sometimes they failed right out of the gate. To transform outcomes, she believes one must have both engineering and sociological aspects. What is the context of the change? She has found that failure comes from having one and not the other. “If you just pay attention to the process side, which many organizations focus on, but not the people side, you will fail,” Jennifer shared.

Jennifer shares a story from her financial services network. Her colleague was head of learning for a bank in New England. The bank was well respected in the area. The bank was trying to improve compliance with the Bank Secrecy Act (BSA) requirements. The BSA is a rule that if a customer deposits $10,000 or more, the bank must report. The Act requires the bank to report to alert that possible fraud and specifically to prevent money laundering. Large deposits are a sign of money laundering. It is very important for the bank to comply, and I cannot imagine any teller not having heard the requirement; it is so fundamental in banking.

Her colleague trained the tellers on the requirement to report any deposit meeting the $10K amount, and yet occurrences of not reporting continued. At one point, management insisted that training was the problem. They were able to prove that the tellers knew the requirement and instead, there was something going on in the branches where the tellers who were failing to comply 100% of the time were working. Applying Principle 1, problem-solving, they found that the root cause was that tellers were very busy at the time of the deposit. They knew they needed to do it, but the branches were simply not giving them enough time.

But most importantly, the bank leaders and managers were not placing an emphasis on the value of reporting. The engineering of the process was never an issue. Tellers knew what to do and had a reasonable process to report, but something else was causing them not to report.

Jennifer's colleague pulled on his contextual sociological skills and suggested to leadership and management that they emphasize “the why” rather than just that reporting needed to be done. Due to the severe consequences of the bank not complying, the bank also included disciplinary consequences two levels up in the organizational structure – not just to the tellers. They had to reinforce that the management needed to comply with telling the why. The bank needed to change the culture so everyone took responsibility, and the tellers would do the verification work required by the Act and not get into trouble.

In healthcare and aviation, we learned about a safety culture and applied it both from an engineering process mindset and also a sociological mindset. A safety culture is one where people feel they will be treated justly and not punished or be reciprocated against. We knew the whole system including context and culture must be evaluated. After initiating the coaching on the why and including leadership in the consequences of noncompliance, the bank's compliance improved greatly.

Jennifer shared a story about noncompliance in a large, very established bank. The bank has been operating for over one hundred years. The bank got into trouble because they overcharged people. This noncompliance event resulted in a person monitoring processes by working at the bank and reviewing how bank employees perform their duties. In automotive, this reaction by regulators is much like one of the Big Three auto manufacturers requiring a third-party inspection on site before parts are shipped to the customer. As head of talent and learning, Jennifer knew the bank needed to change the culture because people needed to know how to whistleblow, and the bank needed a culture of trust before people would feel safe in blowing the whistle on problems. Jennifer teaches the right behaviors plus the right processes. We had to work with the existing culture of fear.

In banking, Jennifer mentioned that about twelve banks run the world's economy, called Globally Systematically Important Banks[5] (G-SIBs). Many of them have been around for years, some for over two-hundred years. "Banking can be very insular resulting in some think they know it all," Jennifer remarked. Jennifer and I both experienced leaders in financial services with little to no experience leading in other industries. Even more surprising to me is that most of the expensive consultants hired by financial services firms have only worked in banking.

An example is in risk management. The risk management techniques in Jennifer's and my consulting experience are immature in some firms. In researching the evolution of federal regulator requirements, hints of the Failure Mode and Effects Analysis (FMEA) are at the origin. I met with the person at the American Bankers Association who developed the risk management module named Risk Control Self-Assessment (RCSA) as it is abbreviated. He agreed that the similarity is clear with the risk management technique that healthcare, aviation, the Department of Defense (DoD), and every industry I worked in called FMEA. I detail FMEA in our first chapter.

He added that he uses FMEA for work on controls in banking, yet banking chose to use the term RCSA instead of the FMEA term. I have no idea why and titling it control self-assessment is not the point. A High Reliability Organization values find the failure mode and its effects on performance. The banking term RCSA wisely includes risk in the name which is the point of understanding risk of failure. But it overemphasizes the value of self-assessment of controls instead of prioritizing the management of reducing the severity of the failure, probability of causes resulting in failure, and the detectability of causes before failure occurs. The RCSA drove many to state a risk and then jump to adding controls. Worse, the pressure to show regulators controls existed drove huge wastes in creating "controls," which were no more than having a meeting about a process and then verifying someone signed off on the minutes where a discussion occurred.

Regardless of what financial services call this risk management technique, the effectiveness is the poorest in managing risk primarily because the firms lack the engineering skills to identify design, process, and system failure potentials, which the FMEA is designed to uncover. Jennifer believes the engineering and the system aspects of sociological skillsets are both key to transforming outcomes, and the engineering skills in managing risk are weak.

Jennifer and I questioned if engineering and sociological skills and application might be their own principle in explaining success in radical changes in outcome. We decided not to deviate from the eight principles because these skills are fundamentals of any business. They do not differentiate organizations that have achieved transformative change from those that have not. In the Eaton example, Eaton had very good engineering and sociological skills across the corporation and the transformations in our unit shared many of the same engineers with other Eaton facilities which struggled.

Reliability

My earlier books cover the term reliability, and I agree 100% with Jennifer's point that engineering and sociological skills are required for reliability and transforming outcomes. Jennifer wonders if financial services firms define reliability well, if at all. She states that a definition could be simple – being accurate is reliability in banking. Drilling down to accuracy, she describes accuracy as, "Am I getting money transferred from X to Y without error?" This process of transferring money is called money movement.

News stories the public sees are a result of not being reliable. The big blow-up in banks is when a failure in ethics, compliance, or money movement occurs. The US Supreme Court said that customers get to keep any money after a bank fails to reliably move money. Money movement is what runs the economy. Banking, and big, big banks, ask how they are moving money between economies. The rest of the KPIs are much less key, to the point they don't care.

Therefore, it seems that transformations in money movement accuracy should be a focus for every financial institution. I don't recall ever being called in to help improve money movement specifically, but our consulting had loads of work around key processes within money movement and especially risk management. Transforming an immature risk management in better understanding risk management is a huge task, going back to the insular nature of banking that Jennifer mentioned.

Employee satisfaction has been a common goal in firms Jennifer has supported. Satisfaction is often a key indicator. Satisfaction is often improved when a firm realizes people want development. Dissatisfaction often takes place in the absence of development. Jennifer describes her job as heavily data driven. She uses data to find the root cause of declining satisfaction scores, often identifying a lack of personal development as the culprit.

In one firm's engagement, she proposed a unifying system that helped with people development. Jennifer is well-versed in a firm's need to translate activities to profitability and she is more successful than others because she can show her impact on profitability. In one firm, its scores improved by 30% by starting an internal academy addressing the people development value to employees.

Sometimes the problem driving the transformation is ill-defined or misdirected. She differentiates her consulting with data analysis and interviews. She strives to use the data to ensure the organization can agree on the problem.

She advises firms resourcing for a transformation to use inside people. But if the firm does not take things off their plate – get a consultant. Jennifer is not a huge fan of transformation offices, as they are often set up to drive efficiency and not change. She, too, sees a lack of correlation with achieving transformations and taking away the transformation potential from the people in the process.

Jennfer says we must tell the problem in terms of a story. Using only data is not the best way to inform and gain consensus. For example, a person says, "Hey, your attrition is 115%." She says it may be better to tell the problem first in terms of a story. That is how you get buy-in, as she has experienced. "Hey, let me tell you about a time when your customer called and here is what happened. Mr. Smith no longer is your customer," is an example of how better to let the story describe the problem. People feel the problem with the story. After using the story, she then presents the data. Not vice versa.

The story and data build credibility for the need for a transformation. Once the need is recognized, the firm can use problem-solving techniques and think through the solution. Once a solution is suggested, create a vision of the solutions. This sets the stage to help them operationalize the solution. This includes estimating the cost, technology, who is needed, etc. Too often the team produces a project plan first, which is wrong. The firm hasn't even defined the problem nor the root cause.

I agree with Jennifer about the project plan. When I see a boatload of project managers and a handful of engineers, I get worried. When I see more people spending time getting their project management certificates than I see engineering degrees and Six Sigma Black Belt certificates, I get more worried. A great engineer is a proven manager of projects. Success in engineering is bringing reliable services and products to market. The greatest project management on earth can at best be described as taking the engineering value and ensuring it came in at cost and on time. Note the absence of also ensuring the project met outcome SMART goals.

Making matters worse is a culture where leaders react quickly to a federal regulator's criticism before conducting a root cause analysis. This is caused by a lack of Principle 1: Developing problem-solving skills. The leader's action is often a "solution-in-mind," and then the very next step is a project plan. Note that the solution in mind is optimistically stated. It most often is a leader's pet project that the leader believes will advance her or him in the organization. Principle 1: Developing problem-solving skills is the best solution for this culture of reactiveness and emphasizing project management without engineering skills and application.

She coaches firms to establish a starting point and to include the outcome in the vision. She asks, "How do we know we transformed without the KPI?" She adds that we don't need 20,000 goals and measures. Everybody should know the correlation between the outcome measure and a process measure. In HR, we are key to influence, but we may not be able to test the correlation of our training and the outcome. If there is a big strong dotted line, maybe a process measure is OK, but I still want the outcome.

How Much of the Organization Do You Need to Achieve a Transformation? If Culture, Everybody

A disciple is needed to help transform. A disciple is one who believes, may be a curmudgeon, and always a representative of a population. The disciple is one who knows where the organization is in relation to the outcome needed. A transformation needs influencers, and they might not be the leaders.

Jennifer sees value in support from at least one leader, a senior-most leader relevant to the outcome. She advises next to put together a core team, including a process engineer, and maybe a project manager, depending on the size of the transformation. This is based on the capabilities of the engineer and team. One cannot overemphasize the importance of communication. Have someone in charge of communications, she suggests, and not necessarily the project manager. Create those stories Jennifer shared about transformations and stories describing the problem.

Jennifer and I both learned behavioral modification using the "ABCs": Antecedents, Behaviors, and Consequences. B.F. Skinner[6] described in Operant Conditioning that behavior, the B, can be changed with Antecedents and Consequences.

1. Antecedent: The trigger or situation that occurs before a behavior.
2. Behavior: The observable action or response.
3. Consequence: The outcome that follows the behavior.

Jennifer compares the ABCs to an addiction model. Jennifer uses the addiction model's steps: Precontemplation, Contemplation, Preparation, Action, Maintenance, Relapse.[7] The hardest is maintenance. Think of a transformation starting with the contemplation of a problem. Then prepare, including getting a team. Then act. Then maintenance – is it a transformation if maintenance is not achieved? By definition, no. It has to sustain. This is the hardest part of the transformation, and often we pack up and go home before this system is put in place. This model reminds us of the importance of setting up an ongoing system of sustainment of the transformed area until it becomes part of the organizational and cultural fabric.

Skills she finds helpful in achieving excellence are: One who has done it, one who communicates well, and one who prioritizes the work well. She agrees it starts with one who can engineer the solution with a sociologist's skillset to help people manage the change.

Summary

This chapter was about Principle 4: Strategize using competitive forces and then match the organizational structure to achieve that strategy. We started the chapter with Chandler's work that a firm is best to start with strategy and not to reorganize and then look at strategy. Too often, organizations are in trouble, and they reorganize only to continue failing. Instead, Motorola and organizations which excel focus first on a strategy. Once a strategy is determined, then and only then will the firm consider its organizational structure and modify or perhaps transform it to achieve the strategy.

Motorola has succeeded for decades, leading its markets and has been rewarded with both market share and recognition for major awards, including the USA's Malcolm Baldrige Award not once but twice with Martin Swarbrick leading the second win.

Jennifer Tice, Ph.D., shares strong evidence from literature and her experience that change is hard. Leaders increase likelihood of transformation by leading change and supporting managing the change with all stakeholders. The ABCs model of behavior reinforcement has been applied throughout my career, and Jennifer adds fuel to the fire in using the ABCs to transform organizations.

Notes

1. Found at https://www.annualreports.com/HostedData/AnnualReports/PDF/NYSE_TWTR_2021.pdf
2. Chandler, Alfred. *Strategy and Structure: Chapters in the History of Industrial Enterprise*, Doubleday, New York, 1962.
3. Source: https://www.nist.gov/baldrige/motorola-inc-commercial-government-and-industrial-solutions-sector-cgis
4. Source: https://www.industryweek.com/archive/article/21941416/motorola-sector-wins-baldrige-award
5. Found at https://www.fsb.org/2023/11/2023-list-of-global-systemically-important-banks-g-sibs/
6. Found at: https://neurolaunch.com/antecedent-behavior-consequence/#google_vignette
7. Found at: https://www.verywellmind.com/the-stages-of-change-model-of-overcoming-addiction-21961

Chapter 4

Transforming Quality

SKF wants to expand its Six Sigma successes and it's not about the krona, it's about customers.

Tom Johnstone, former CEO of SKF

Background

Industry: Manufacturing/Distribution Automotive, Aerospace, Defense, Racing Components, Construction Equipment, Industrial
Where: Gothenburg, Sweden, with SKF US Seals Headquarters in Elgin, IL, USA.
Organization: Manufacturing
Markets served by this facility: The Americas (primarily)
Products/Services: Automotive, Truck, and Commercial Seals primarily.

History

SKF is a global leader in bearings and seals. SKF acquired Chicago Rawhide (CR) to vertically integrate seals with SKF's bearing and wheel unit capabilities. Ever since the 1920s, Ford and other automotive manufacturers have been installing seals to retain the oil or grease necessary for bearings which are critical for rotating axles to prevent failure. The other benefit of the oil seal was to keep the streets and roads a bit cleaner. Prior to the use of an oil seal, the Model T and other vehicles basically had a cup to retain the grease

DOI: 10.4324/9781032639574-4

which dripped oil on the rotating parts and too often, the streets. Today, SKF's bearings are installed in anything that rotates, including jet engines, wheels on your car, engines, and military equipment, to name a few applications. CR's seal is an engineering marvel, with surfaces so finely produced and vital to retaining the oil that the quality cannot be measured with the naked eye. SKF pioneered reliability concepts to a next-level focus on quality and a customer-first mindset. Quality is still its competitive advantage.

Chicago Rawhide was purchased by SKF in 1990 because SKF wanted to own the product that protected its bearings. Chicago Rawhide was one of the oldest, most experienced seal manufacturers in the world, and its emphasis on reliability was a perfect strategic fit for SKF – the world leader in highly reliable bearings. In 2001, I was recruited to lead Quality by two former Eaton executives, George Dettloff and Alan Houser. After 21 years at Eaton, and I think because of the transformation success Al and I had, they asked me to help them build Chicago Rawhide better, as we did at Eaton. At the time of our onboarding discussions, they debated having me lead quality or supply chain and eventually decided they needed me most to improve the quality of its products. SKF's and Chicago Rawhide's focus on quality was exciting to me, having been very focused lately at Eaton on profitability improvement. The product was still a market leader but the gap was a strategic one. The bar was continuing to be raised by powerful customers and Claes, George, and Al found CR's Quality needing to contribute more to improve reliability and upgrade CR's problem-solving capabilities across all of its products.

Leader Bios (During Transformation)

Corporate CEO – Tom Johnstone
SKF Chicago Rawhide Seals President – George Dettloff
Al Houser – Vice President (VP) of Operations
Group Leader for Quality - Claes Rehmberg
Vice President of Quality, Seals America – Richard Morrow. I reported directly into the CR Seals Unit with a dotted line to Claes.

Pre-Transformation State of Quality

Claes Rehmberg took me under his wing and expressed his appreciation that George and Al valued quality. He had been frustrated with Chicago Rawhide over its lack of quality initiatives universally accepted globally in SKF's other divisions. Claes, George, and Al agreed his concern was valid because SKF's main products were bearings, and the seal which our division manufactured and SKF wanted more synergy from the purchase of this critical component. Quality leadership was both SKF and CR's market advantage.

There was a lack of interest in taking advantage of the SKF Quality Group prior to George and Al joining SKF in Chicago Rawhide. Group Quality was based at SKF Headquarters in Gothenburg, Sweden, but representatives from across SKF's businesses were part of this empowered group. I had nothing to lose by listening and learning about this entirely new-to-me product line and automotive and other vehicle and equipment markets. George, Al, and I wanted our division to excel. At the start, I did not know how much improvement was needed other than that we had some quality and operations issues. I found out quickly during my first plant tour.

The automotive industry is a tough industry. Intense cost pressure, high volume, and severe consequences for poor quality demand high reliability. Using Michael Porter's Five Competitive Forces concept, the customers held the power. Ford, GM, Chrysler, Toyota, and others had plenty of companies wanting to supply products, including seals and bearings, so quality and price had to be competitive and differentiating. Caterpillar, John Deere, and others in the Industrial markets held the same sway that the automotive industry held.

My first issue to tackle was a Zero Kilometer Failure. It was a new term to me and I learned it was a forbidden quality failure. Fortunately, CR had very few of these and few enough it was not a Key Performance Indicator. CR's high reliability made CR the market leader it was. These failures are when components installed in vehicles fail before the vehicle leaves the factory. It is important at the beginning of a story to share the KPIs and key measures because this book is about moving those needles. Measuring the number of zero kilometer failures is not what you do because having one is a result of more likely contributing factors that should be measured to prevent the zero kilometer failure. I will detail more about these types of failures in my next story while in Motorola and in the healthcare stories of transformations.

I learned about one product that resulted in these failures and it created very bad days at CR. I gained a respect for the fact that I had a lot to learn about the auto industry. At Eaton Electrical, the customers were many and the market was fragmented and thus no one customer had the power over us compared to the automotive industry where very few auto companies had immense power over its suppliers. A Quality organization in electrical safety products interfaced with its production and design teams most often. Also critical was a quality organization which could work with electrical utilities, regulatory agencies, and distributors. The customer base was very fragmented meaning no one customer had as much of a voice compared to CR's business. Our customers were primarily the electrical distributor, electrician, or homeowner installing or benefitting from our products. At CR, the strategy was about winning and keeping sales to the vehicle manufacturer and thus we needed an organization that could translate product design and sales requirements into manufacturing requirements directly with the customer, not only within CR. Customers is plural because a vehicle manufacturer might not buy our seal directly but via a much more complex assembly manufactured by multiple suppliers. An example is our seal might be shipped to a wheel or axle manufacturer. This assembly would then be shipped to another larger component supplier who next might ship to the vehicle final assembly.

We needed a Quality organization to solve problems throughout this complex supply chain and many suppliers. George and Al asked me to meet Claes and bring back Claes' perspective of Chicago Rawhide. We then needed to decide our KPIs relative to our role in Quality.

My first trip to Gothenburg was the first trip to Sweden and meeting leaders in SKF's world headquarters. As VP of Quality for Seals in America, I worked under Claes with a dotted line reporting structure which SKF wanted because Claes had a lot riding on me to bring CR into the fold on quality. Claes picked me up from the hotel but not before I learned a few phrases in Swedish. I'll never forget his look at me when I greeted him with saying good morning in Swedish. He surely did not understand me, laughed, and said stick with English. Claes was one of the most intelligent and fair leaders I had the pleasure of working with. Claes took me under his wing early on and later reciprocated by interrupting his work at HQ in Gothenburg to meet me in our offices during my first weeks.

I began to learn high reliability and the fruits of being the best by far in quality. How good was SKF? SKF was the chosen supplier to the Ferrari F1 Race Team for any race car component that SKF manufactured. Being the chosen supplier for the most technologically advanced race car and one of its best teams is evidence enough. One of the reasons SKF earned that market is the first SKF invented quality program he shared with me. SKF named it "Zero Defects."

Zero Defects Program

Claes was quick to let me know CR had not one facility or even one product line participating. Most every, if not all, SKF factories had been participating for years. Claes had a motive in traveling so soon to meet with me, I discovered. He wanted Chicago Rawhide to join the corporate-wide key Quality Programs that CR's earlier leadership had ignored. Claes was happy with George and Al joining, and he saw the opportunity to teach this new guy SKF Quality and the culture that made SKF the world leader in bearings for nearly one hundred years. At the time, I had no idea where specifically I needed to work, nor how much change or transformation would be my work. Al had suggested I needed to start making major changes in the Quality organization knowing the strategy is to accelerate our quality improvement and gain synergy from Claes' Group Quality practices.

Zero defects, the program, was a success for SKF because it measured outcomes, and these outcomes were a KPI of our customers including Ford, GM, and Chrysler, as well as John Deere, Caterpillar Tractor Company, and many others. Zero Defect as a measure equates to the customer receiving no defects from CR. In Chapter 1 we detailed how important the measurement system is to knowing the truth. SKF had demanding automotive customers, who did not seem to hesitate to complain, as I learned. But SKF was dependent on the customer to let it know if SKF shipped a defective bearing or seal to its site. I will explain by detailing the measurement system but suffice it to say achieving ZD was measured by receiving no complaints on product quality from the customer.

Zero Defect was also a cultural measure. Participation was measured and each facility was evaluated on how many product lines had achieved ZD for a year. The ZD Awards were given to the employees who achieved this recognition of high reliability. To know more about reliability and leading an organization to excel in reliability, consider reading my book, "*Leading High Reliability Organizations in Healthcare*." The book is written for leaders in any industry.

SKF chose a proxy measure to knowing truly if any component was faulty because having a KPI that relied on the customer for us to measure is a bit much to ask of the customer. But the ZD measurement system also gave us a measure of our relationship with a customer. The actual measure SKF used was from the voice of the customer. Zero Defect is achieved if SKF received no complaints about quality for the prior year. An award would be earned from Claes and the Corporate Group for every year a production line received zero complaints on quality. A production line was defined by the facility in how it organized its people and equipment to produce products within a production line. Thinking of the cellular flow success at Lincoln, each cell would be eligible for the award. At CR, we didn't have U-shaped cells when I joined because it was like Lincoln Plant's manufacturing functional layout prior to the transformation. CR did not have the manufacturing transformation that Eaton had. Very little changed in the manufacturing and production organization because Chicago Rawhide was mostly organized by product line with little crossline manufacturing commonality. We provided more definition to the channel organization which was needed more formally to participate in the SKF ZD program. Setting the stage for our Quality organization transformation, I went back to our plants and confirmed none of our plants were participating in the ZD program. Claes and I did not know why, but I promised to find out and get us in the program. George and Al had little knowledge of the program in their early days, so I took it on for us.

The ZD measure seemed to alert us if we had a defect. As I met our customers, I found no customer reluctant to tell me something was wrong. Therefore, I trusted the measure gave us the essence that we were very good in quality – or not if we received a complaint. SKF had strict guidelines to judge a complaint, and this was also a subject of concern that CR was using the same rules.

I also used the measure to assess the relationship. If a customer thinks SKF is the best supplier on earth, I knew there was a risk that if we had a product line ship bad parts, the customer may not tell us. I was concerned that our good reputation might prevent knowing we had a failure. But if a customer issued complaints, and especially increased its rate of complaining, it was a signal to Principle 5: Engage and Go See. The customer was telling us something, and we needed to find out what and fix it.

International Organization for Standardization and What It Reinforced Explained

What Al also tasked me with for our Seals Division was to manage the deluge of office visits from my direct report who led the ISO 9000[1] (The International Organization for Standardization) quality program. This leader was at his door often, wanting Al to force plants to pay more attention to the Quality Department and ISO programs. ISO is a significant force in the auto industry for some manufacturers, and this pressure was a root cause of some of the issues CR was having. We needed big changes in our organization which was organized around ISO inspections and reporting – not always our customers' needs.

The International Organization for Standardization is an inspection program where participating customers pay for third party ISO-trained inspectors to come and certify that your facility, not products, meets the ISO standards. I emphasize ISO-certified products, not ISO-certified companies. My point is that ISO does not attempt to assess the leadership and organization, implying anything the company does meets its standards. ISO is wise to assess the quality program against its standards. From the ISO website products, services, or systems meet standards.

From the ISO website:

ISO/TS 16949 is an ISO technical specification for automotive sector quality management systems. It was first developed in 1999 by the IATF in conjunction with ISO's technical committee for quality management, ISO/TC 176. Since then, it has risen to be one of the most widely used International Standards in the automotive industry and aims to harmonize the different assessment and certification systems in the global automotive supply chain.

ISO states the benefits to the auto companies and others requiring its suppliers to become certified to the ISO standards:

Why is ISO 9001 important?

With more than one million certificates issued to organizations in 189 countries, ISO 9001 is the most widely used quality management standard in the world. Within the ISO 9000 family, which defines seven quality management principles including a strong customer focus and continual improvement, ISO 9001 is the only standard that can be certified to (though certification is not mandatory).

Business benefits include:

- *Customer confidence: The standard ensures that organizations have robust quality control processes in place, leading to increased customer trust and satisfaction*
- *Effective complaint resolution: ISO 9001 offers guidelines for resolving customer complaints efficiently, contributing to timely and satisfactory problem-solving*

- *Process improvement: The standard helps identify and eliminate inefficiencies, reduce waste, streamline operations, and promote informed decision-making, resulting in cost savings and better outcome*
- *Ongoing optimization: Regular audits and reviews encouraged by ISO 9001 enable organizations to continually refine their quality management systems, stay competitive, and achieve long-term success*

Note that nowhere does it state that the parts purchased meet the buyer's requirements. Nor would I expect. ISO 9001 certifies that the Quality Management meets the standards. The hope is that a company passing the ISO certification by a third party will ship good parts.

From the ISO website: *"Certification is the provision by an independent body of written assurance (a certificate) that the product, process, service, or system in question meets specific requirements. Certification is also known as third-party conformity assessment.*

ISO's website About Us page section states ISO is:

Practical solutions for real-world problems

ISO, the International Organization for Standardization, brings global experts together to agree on the best ways of doing things – for anything from making a product to managing a process. As one of the oldest nongovernmental international organizations, ISO has enabled trade and cooperation between people and companies around the world over since 1946. The International Standards published by ISO serve to make lives easier, safer, and better.

There you have it. Straight from ISO's website.

I asked if ISO is such a no-brainer, then why did Ford, GM, and Chrysler not require their facilities to be certified? At the time, the Big Three did not have many of their facilities achieving ISO certification. Al had been deluged before I joined with my direct report's concerns that plants were not achieving ISO standards and might fail the inspections that occur from an ISO-registered third-party firm. Yes, we pay a third party to judge if we are compliant with global standards.

For those who know Deming's work, are you thinking Deming would disapprove paying third party to come and inspect? Deming warned management in the automotive industry, the same industry we were in, that inspection is not the answer to quality. ISO is not shy to state that it is about inspecting to see if the firm's quality program meets the standards that this international body has imposed. Note that it is about the quality program, not the quality of the parts we made, that ISO standards are written to cover.

I found it odd and disheartening that the very industry that Deming was berating for relying on inspection, demanded suppliers achieve ISO. Many Japanese firms followed Deming's guidance to design in quality and rely on statistical process control over trying to catch defects before they escape to the customer. US auto manufacturers required its suppliers to follow ISO and pay third-party inspection firms. How did the auto industry fall into this practice?

Cost savings, I believe, is the reason. I believe the auto industry initially saw ISO as a way to reduce its own inspection costs of suppliers. Ford, GM, and Chrysler shared the same suppliers often and the Seals Division would routinely be answering annually for each customer, if not more frequently, about our quality program. We also would host the customers' Supplier Quality teams which visited our many facilities. This cost the "Big Three," as they were labeled, significantly. ISO became a way to "outsource" the wasteful inspection each of them was paying for, shifting the cost of these inspections back onto the supplier, CR, and allowing the Big Three to eliminate many of their employees in Supplier Quality.

Despite the Big Three's history of competing among themselves and aside from ISO, they joined together and developed some of the best quality practices, and the benefits to us suppliers were tremendous. Risk management practices are one example.

The Failure Mode and Effects Analysis (FMEA) is instrumental in risk management across the auto industry. Using FMEA not only achieved higher product quality for the auto manufacturers but it also became the standard for identifying risks and eliminating or mitigate the highest priority. The healthcare industry later adopted FMEA or similar practices, improving surgical safety and other healthcare risks to patients. As a supplier, we could invest in learning FMEA and be assured we would satisfy the Big Three's risk management process requirements and avoid the complexity of multiple risk management techniques. The FMEA was used by the Big Three, and no ISO oversight or third-party costs were required.

I write about the Big Three, but there are many other auto manufacturing companies. I was not surprised to learn that not all of our major vehicle manufacturing customers required passing ISO inspections. Ford, GM, and Chrysler required ISO, but Toyota did not. Toyota had its own requirements that primarily guided suppliers in utilizing design and process reliability practices. Toyota did not require us to pay for inspection.

The ISO 9001 or its automotive-specific TS16949 version not certifying outcomes or good parts. It is not an outcome measure – it is a process measure. It is trying to measure if your quality management process is effective. Essentially, certification assesses if you have met the ISO standards of what constitutes a good quality management system. Here is the silliness of one of its standards.

The ISO required us to have a quality manual. I found we had one. Pages and pages I found when my direct report delivered to me our quality manual. I asked her what specifically ISO requires in the quality manual. I got a blank stare. What I found was a "check-the-box" standard. We had passed inspections prior to my arrival with this gob of pages.

Even though ISO touts that complying with its ISO standard will result in more satisfied customers, the evidence was lacking that we had happier customers since first being certified to the ISO standards. In fact, I am pretty sure George and Al would not have recruited me for Quality choosing a different issue for me to tackle, such as the supply chain. It had some significant opportunities Al and I found later.

Claes and SKF long ago had facilities certified in ISO but shifted resources in their SKF plants' Quality organizations to ZD and other measures of outcome. We valued the customer-voice, not standards that often had no data showing correlation with outcomes customers wanted.

This transformation story is not about our parts improving in quality, although our plants did improve. This story is about transforming the quality culture – the mindset and how to improve quality. The transformation had not occurred from ISO efforts. Here is what happened instead.

SKF Seals Division was heavily invested in humans inspecting quality. We were missing statistical process control methods, and my team was all stationed in Elgin, Illinois, with dotted line reports in each of the plants. The quality managers in each plant reported to the plant manager at the facility. This decentralized organization remained, and anything different was not proposed by me. SKF was successful in its matrix-style organization, and I was a part of it. As a Division VP of Quality, SKF might have required me to report directly to Claes, the corporate leader of quality, but I did not.

The essence of quality management as I knew it and practiced it was to empower those on the frontline, arming them with the tools and skills they need and respecting the closeness of the leadership team to the operation. The transformation we journeyed on was about openness to better quality management practices, not the organizational structure as it was with Eaton's Lincoln plant.

Al hosted me on a quick tour of our facilities soon after joining. I found the same practices in manufacturing, including batch processes of functionally aligned departments instead of continuous quick flow and cellular manufacturing but what was also in common with CR's facilities was the escape from union collective bargaining. The problems and solutions in this book thus help most anyone, regardless of company within the industry. Even better is the value of the principles regardless of industry.

Years before Al, George, and I joined CR, CR's leadership chose to escape the collective bargaining facility in Elgin and set up smaller facilities, hoping to cut costs in the highly competitive auto supply industry. Labor cost was a major reason to relocate. CR was now in multiple sites in remote areas of Oklahoma and other states. Just like Eaton, the company started the exodus to lower costs. Again, labor cost was a major factor and the desire to leave the collective bargaining union facility. Like Eaton, it chose less populated rural areas. CR made a more complex move than Eaton's move. CR split one facility into multiple smaller sites, all very far from each other.

But not everything moved. A seal's main "ingredient" is the rubber compound. Rubber compounding remained at the old Elgin facility along with some manufacturing. So, CR shifted labor costs to remote areas, but now it was incurring shipping and handling costs of the rubber compounds to these remote facilities. Eaton moved 100% of the Wisconsin facility, but the similarities among manufacturing are proven again, which is why this book's solutions should support most manufacturing companies' needs in transforming success.

The CR plant managers seemed open to the position of VP of Quality for the Seals America business unit. My position did not exist before. The plants received guidance and instruction in quality principles from my team before I joined, but I soon learned my group's main role was to support them in achieving ISO certification. Not exciting to say the least, and Al had seen no value in ISO; thus, I soon recognized my role and my team's role had to shift to something more valuable. The strategy was not to achieve ISO. It was to better compete on the outcome KPI of quality. ISO was at best a means to better quality.

The plants also used my team to handle complaints from major customers when quality issues arose. I found this interesting because my team had no contribution to a failure of products made in these plants, yet we were the ones who hopped on a plane to Detroit or wherever the customer wanted us to explain what CR was doing to solve the problem.

Missing in the balance of our contribution to our plants from my team's roles was skill development in quality and support on the floor in design and process improvement. At Eaton, we had conferences and speakers, including leaders in quality and among our customers. Ford, too, was a customer of Eaton Automotive, and I heard Ford's Quality Executive in the late 1990s speak on Ford's shift in quality with suppliers to one of support and collaboration instead of the often aggressive relationship focused on punishment if quality was not meeting Ford's requirements. Interestingly, Ford, just before I started at CR, also found that a Six Sigma mindset[2] would improve quality, whereas its ISO mandate was not getting the outcomes it wanted.

CR's plants were my team's customers and I saw their needs immediately. We needed to shift the focus from mainly supporting/maintaining ISO certification to the role of supporting quality improvement beginning with offering skill development in achieving higher reliability. Principle #1. The cost of poor quality, a common performance indicator promoted by Deming, Juran, and Crosby, was a metric we needed to leverage. An example is the cost of shipping poor quality to a major vehicle manufacturer follows.

In our main plant in Elgin, CR had Level three inspection required by GM for poor quality. Level three is costly. Level three inspection required CR to pay for a third party to come into our facilities and inspect 100% of the parts before shipping them to GM's factories.

GM had attempted to get CR to fix issues with a product we sent to GM, but to no avail. Level three was a desperation attempt to contain quality issues from reaching GM. GM shifted its inspection of our product back onto us, and worse, it did not trust us to inspect products ourselves by requiring CR to pay for a third party to literally be in our plant inspecting our product before shipping to GM.

In perspective, and to be fair, CR seals were considered high quality, which is why Ford, GM, and Chrysler, including John Deere, Caterpillar, and countless other great firms, bought our seals. But we needed to improve to stay competitive, and my job was to improve the quality. The first tour convinced me that my team could make the most by offering skill development to the plants in quality practices, which Eaton was very good at. Al and I wanted to respect the plants' autonomy, and we had no reason to try to manage them from Elgin. In fact, we couldn't because of the culture and remoteness. We would be worn out traveling with multiple airplane connections and typically a 2-hour drive from the nearest airport. CR certainly accomplished finding remote areas!

CR had remnants of quality programs including Total Quality Management but the outcomes as shared above, were not where we needed them to be. CR was behind in quality science practices, including statistical process control, which our customers knew and promoted within their sites and with suppliers. Problem-solving skills were the basic fire-fighting methods of jumping in when parts were failing, but little in problem-prevention. Failure Mode and Effects Analysis was taught and used to meet Ford's requirements in new product design, and the auto industry often required an FMEA before shipping the first part.

The fact that we had quality problems suggested something was missing in the value of the FMEA, which should eliminate or mitigate failures in process, design, and system. I found the gap to be in the use of the FMEA's findings. Doing an FMEA worksheet is tedious, but to invest in doing one and then not utilizing the prioritization discovery of risks most important to address because of the severity, occurrence of risk, and detectability is wasteful. I could not see evidence of leadership supporting the findings in the FMEA even when we had failures. Long ago I learned the first thing to ask for in a failure or near-failure is the FMEA and what was missed in the FMEA. This single practice transforms the value of the FMEA effort. As the head of quality, I had to start showing leadership, and my fellow leaders quickly learned that the plant better get Rick the FMEA quickly, or they will see Rick more than they want.

The Principles to Achieve Excellence and Transformational Improvements

I use the Principles to share a baseline of what Al, George, and I started with at CR:

Principle 1: Develop problem-solving skills – There was no evidence of a training program from my team for the plants other than in ISO certification. Claes had offered training, but I could not find evidence of attendance.

Principle 2: Utilize Measure, Manage to the measure, and Making it easier (3Ms). CR measured ISO certification and outcomes such as complaints from customers. It was weak in measuring the process variables that were root causes of failure. Process control was primarily through inspection vs. statistical. We measured ISO certifications and outcomes of failure with ZD but we missed the process control techniques that prevent failure.

Principle 3: SMART with radical goals. Claes had SMART goals for CR quality but little evidence that any facility knew them, such as the program called ZD or practicing behaviors to achieve the goals.

Principle 4: Competitive force strategy and organizational structure match. Porter's Five Forces were very clearly proven. In automotive, the customer was the driving force. Cost reduction and quality were paramount to them, with innovation fortunately high on their wishes and CR developed many great innovations. Business could be lost quickly from poor quality and the force from existing competitors was extremely strong. Our organization was very typical in manufacturing, with some central group (mine) but most decisions were made locally.

Principle 5: Engage – Go see firsthand. I did not hear of my team going to the plants except for ISO training or recovery from a major quality issue. None of the trips seemed proactive and to support the plants in quality skills.

Principle 6: Manage risk. The use of risk management was primarily to check the box to comply with large customers who demanded an FMEA.

Principle 7: Celebrate quick wins. There was no unifying quality program that reinforced quality improvement well, nor was there a gathering of quality professionals for much other than ISO.

Principle 8: Keep utilizing the 3Ms. I needed to focus on them knowing and utilizing the 3Ms first.

Skill Development Leading to Excel

As mentioned, the skill development in quality practices was minimal despite Claes' and his team's knowledge and expertise. CR just hadn't taken advantage of SKF's quality offerings, including the ZD program and its skill training. One of my directors would attend Claes' group meetings, but I could not see much evidence of putting the meeting's value to work for CR other than ISO support to the plants that was shared at these globally attended meetings.

I heard, though, that my peers across the globe were interested in Six Sigma, and in my first meeting, Claes had an agenda item to learn more knowing my experience using Six Sigma. This humility from Claes and my peers, with much more experience than I in SKF and in the science of quality, made me a fan of this group, but I needed more from them. Attending were leaders in quality across SKF's many businesses, including the bearings and seals group that earned 100% of Ferrari's F1 team's business[3]. If SKF made it, this team bought it from SKF. Scuderia Ferrari, one of the most celebrated teams in Formula 1, has competed in every championship. Since the F1 circuit was founded in 1947, SKF has been one of Scuderia Ferrari's technical partners. I wanted to know more about how SKF earned such an honor in supplying Scuderia in the most technologically advanced car racing circuit in the world. Today, the Scuderia Ferrari car is fitted with around three hundred fully customized SKF bearings and condition monitoring solutions.

At my first SKF global leader meeting with my peers, and I say that humbly, I found every leader very personable and inviting. These were leaders from organizations which excelled in customer satisfaction and held many awards in SKF's ZD program. I knew from the introductions that SKF was going to expose me to many new ideas and a global culture. Each person introduced himself or herself in English, not their native language, and most surprisingly, volunteered their ages. I was not accustomed to that level of openness and, although frowned upon by many in the USA, it indicated not only a culture of openness but it also clued me into the long years of experience in the room.

Juergen Schulteis, leader of quality in Schweinfurt, Germany, was one of the first to introduce himself, followed by Hans Kirch from the Seals Division in Germany. Hans, Juergen, and I would have many conversations in the years that followed because their units led much of SKF in quality, and Hans' unit made similar products to what CR produced. Principle 5: Go See was high on my priority list. Bearings were instrumental in the war effort during World War II, and Schweinfurt was heavily bombed to knock out the bearing production. SKF had earlier shifted away from selling bearings to the German war effort and later helped Germany rebuild, as did America. I sat there wondering how I would be accepted with both Germany and Italy represented. Silvio Rubatto, Quality Leader in Italy at the time, and I continue to be friends, and he led Quality for all of SKF in Claes' role after Claes retired. Silvio was one of the most inquisitive leaders, and I think represents SKF's culture of humility and continuous learning. This leads us to Principle 1: Develop problem-solving skills.

Claes asked me to cover my background in Six Sigma and I expected criticism on this so-called American quality program and a program that SKF had avoided across the globe. Instead, I found the same openness and inquisitiveness displayed by Claes when we first met, and from the very beginning of this first meeting for me with true leaders in quality.

At the time, I did not know when my training and problem-solving skills at Eaton would be used or how much because I did not know CR well yet. This meeting with Group Quality Leaders came very early, and I was intent on listening and learning from them. I did not want to be the "Loud American," a term many overseas used to describe us.

The meeting was consumed mostly with ISO issues as some of the facilities represented were to undergo their ISO certification visits. I learned that our role was very much to learn and to share with our counterparts what the third parties were finding weak and how to strengthen our compliance with the ISO standards. Even though I was on the leadership team at the Eaton Lincoln Plant for ISO certification, which is another common facet shared with many in the manufacturing sector, I did not have experience working with my peers across other Eaton facilities and definitely not globally. SKF's problem-solving skills development was truly global, and I learned much about ISO from this first session that I would take back.

But in perspective, I never became the expert in ISO that each of my colleagues was. I was the person sitting quietly in every ISO agenda item during the years I worked at SKF. I had reports to give and shared what our facilities learned and the problems we faced getting recertified, but there was never any pressure to "talk ISO" more. This acceptance was Claes' leadership skill in capitalizing on each person's contribution while not burdening any of us with matters that most in each of our countries and facilities.

Back home in the USA, our problems were becoming visible in both ISO inspections and, more importantly, with our customers. We needed to radically improve our Quality strategy and then our quality organization's mission and focus. We needed to shift from inspecting and being insular within CR to High Reliability and become part of the SKF Quality group. I am most proud that this organizational transformation included the same people. One of my directors showed more interest in the required ISO support. I did not need two directors focused on ISO compliance. I could rely on one of my direct reports to handle the ISO certification, thankfully, and she loved the role of ISO coach. One other director was excited about Six Sigma so he became my Quality Leader for everything not ISO related, which gave CR a significant improvement in the Quality Science skill development across CR for the first time. Carolyn and Ernie in turn took their organizations and shifted roles to the strategy of high reliability, utilizing SKF's many resources, and both became two of our first Black Belts to lead problem-solving across the plants and suppliers. They became much more skilled in the science of quality. I pulled Ernie and Carolyn together, and we decided to begin their training in Six Sigma, with Carolyn taking prime responsibility for ISO support in the plants and Ernie focusing on the major quality problems. This division of responsibilities continued well after I left and served the Seals Division well.

Quality Science is the science of quality. I like this definition from a firm, Pathway for Patient Health[4]: *The holistic approach of our Quality Science Education program combines the science, regulatory, and business acumen needed to:*

- *Mobilize enterprise-wide quality effectiveness grounded in science, data, stakeholder awareness, and regulatory intelligence*
- *Proactively anticipate and manage risk, optimize value, and provide objectivity*
- *Understand the business in which employees operate and how to positively affect the outcome*
- *Establish innovative systems to increase the right-first-time rate of cross-functional stakeholders, thus bolstering consumer and regulatory confidence in product safety, efficacy, and intended use*

The Quality Science Education from this firm's curriculum is not a "training" program; it states,

> instead, it is a rigorous, intensive plan of study grounded in science that yields career-ready professionals who are adept in the field of quality science. Graduates of the Quality Science Education program enter their desired profession with the skills necessary to increase the assurance of product quality, safety, and efficacy.

Note that Principles 1, 2, 3, 4, and 6 of problem-solving skills, 3Ms, goals in quality, organizational structure, and risk management are in this definition. SKF's ZD program also displayed these principles practiced by firms who achieved transformations in quality, and Claes' regular meetings unknowingly but purposely, covered status in each of these principles.

Ernie excelled in Six Sigma and would become the first Master Black Belt trained in SKF. He continued solving its most complex problems after I left SKF for Motorola. He argued that CR needed something beyond ISO because of failures he was seeing despite having achieved ISO certification years before. I invited him to a meeting with Al and George to share Ernie's concerns about poor quality and his interest in doing something different to solve the issues. Al and George closed the meeting by thanking Ernie and giving us the green light to do what we needed to improve quality.

Let us take two stories involving a lack of quality to show the transformation in the USA Quality organization, which started and achieved radical success. The details of the problems will be masked and intermingled to best tell the story. The story ends with success in solving the issues, and the teams found that key multiple root causes were caused by suppliers other than CR. This transformation illustrates how to excel by transforming an organization and is not a story of transforming the quality of a product.

Before we solved these problems, we trained ourselves to solve problems. Six Sigma, the Motorola program initiated because of Principle 4: Competitive force strategy and organization structure match. The famous quote from Motorola that it was losing market share, "because our quality stinks," initiated a culture change in Motorola to design and produce products that exceeded its competitors' quality and take back the market it led in Pagers. Mikel Harry's interview in my book, "*Leading High Reliability Organizations in Healthcare*," confirmed the story and the beginning of Motorola's Six Sigma to lead in quality and gain back the market share, beginning with the design of the "Badger" pager.

Ernie, Carolyn, and their direct reports began their Six Sigma training, and the culture changes became evident from the first session. They spoke in new terms of defects per million, data-driven quality measures, and Six Sigma quality. Culture is hard to measure, but listening to the conversations is evidence that the culture is changing. These terms and concepts were early signs that our culture in quality was already changing. Transforming the language used was another sign the organization was transforming.

I know some of our teammates were reluctant to learn Six Sigma, and it would affect applying the learning, so I practiced Principle 5: Engage and Go See often. I could sense the obvious resistance and know I most likely missed many of the passive-aggressive behaviors, but in the end, even the most ardent resisters changed not only their language but solved problems better and faster than before. Even our ISO certification efforts became easier because our facilities would later boast of having Six Sigma Black Belts and the extensive training occurring every day on the job as our quality professionals instructed frontline people as well as leaders in these remote plants about Six Sigma and its benefits in solving even the most complex problems.

The language among leaders was changing in the same way as my team's language changed. My team started getting invited to come to some plants and help them with their biggest issues. Before our Six Sigma launch, we were not exactly high in demand. Most of the demand was for support in the periodic ISO recertification and not so much to help them solve their customer issues. In fact, the team before I joined were seldom asked to come and help. Now, they were on planes going to plants and suppliers.

Joe reported to Ernie and was responsible for supporting some of the biggest issues. Joe took Six Sigma training and immediately started applying it to the problems mentioned. He helped the production and design areas with his new skills, and CR achieved success in both issues.

Claes was kept aware of CR's customer issues, and he took full advantage of our need to improve customer satisfaction with SKF's ZD. CR now, finally, had a culture that accepted this program's value, and Claes came and was instrumental in delivering the training and program leadership everyone in CR needed, including me. I had to learn how to administer it.

George and Al provided the support we needed to open the door at our plants to participate in the ZD program. The very measure of ZD, the plant managers knew, would expose quality defects that they might have been able to hide from Al and George before. So, it was a big change and win for the plants to participate. Any product line not receiving a ZD Award meant failure once a product line started participating. The fact that anyone would anyone voluntarily participate, as it was voluntary at the time voluntarily, speaks volumes about the culture change. Our definition of a transformation is that a level of performance was achieved that had never been before. Jumping to the time element, years after I left SKF, these same plants were still participating.

Within a year, CR had its first product lines achieving the SKF ZD Award. Honestly, these plants were probably achieving ZD before, but the culture never cared nor allowed participation. Thanks to the celebration built into the ZD program, we now practiced the principle to celebrate which motivated the frontline and plant management to continuously improve. It was a cultural and organizational transformation as judged by the product quality, which probably did not always transform – it was the culture that improved radically.

Claes and the CEO at the time, Tom Johnstone, saw the transformation occurring in our Seals Division and invited me to speak on Six Sigma with the Corporate Officers. Tom's interest was whether SKF's other businesses and other countries could benefit from Six Sigma. Tom heard from Claes about the change in CR's acceptance of the SKF ZD program and how the

Quality team took responsibility to develop skills in quality and not just act as an ISO support group.

The leaders in the meeting expressed interest in Six Sigma after seeing our success and hearing the story of shifting resources toward product quality. Some businesses had similar concerns about the Quality organization's resources being poured into efforts to recertify in a program that was essentially a barrier to entry, with some customers checked off but not much in competing on quality.

I and my team were now challenged to help Claes roll out Six Sigma worldwide. We did this with each of the countries' quality leaders joining the first SKF global Six Sigma Black Belt training, who would become the Master Black Belts in SKF. I can't say SKF transformed every quality organization because SKF was already a world leader and literally "wrote the book" on reliability because of successes like the Scuderia F1 Race team's partnership. What it did, though, was improve problem-solving ability when multiple SKF sites might be contributing to customer failures from complex multi-product assemblies.

It is not enough to have a cultural transformation in a global business like SKF. In this story, one SKF business group provides one component, another group that may be in a different country supplies a second, and third-party suppliers may take these components and assemble them with components made in its factories. Then, the final manufacturing may take our and the third-party's assembly and incorporate it in yet another more complex system – the vehicle.

In this story, there were vehicle issues that I measured to occur very infrequently, about 0.001% of the time. But when they occurred, the outcome was significant. SKF utilized its new problem-solving skills in searching for the root causes. Organizationally, this failure mode exposed some cultural "opportunities" because of reluctance from a facility manager to support any root cause coming from the plant.

There was finger-pointing among every organization involved that might possibly contribute to the failure. The failure could have been caused across the supply chain in four major organizations, and processes that could occur in the typical vehicle maintenance cycle were considered the most likely sources of the root causes. The organizations were CR, which manufactured the seal in one location, and SKF, organization #2, which assembled the seal into its component. The third organization was our customer, which assembled SKF's assembly into a larger assembly. Even customers were involved because their installation could damage the assembly. Thus, we had four different cultures to investigate.

Principle 5: Engage and Go See is the best way to find the root causes. Notice that I use the plural because our experience suggests no one root cause usually results in failures. It's the Swiss Cheese Model that James Reason[5] borrowed to explain how failures occur in complex systems. CR, SKF, our customer, and the final customer all had defenses to reduce the chance a mistake or defect would cause a failure occurring. James Reason suggests thinking of slices of Swiss cheese, with each slice being the defense each of the companies had to prevent a failure from escaping their defense and affecting the vehicle owner. But like Swiss cheese, there are "holes" in every defense, and there is a possibility that all those holes line up 1 day and the failure occurs despite all the defenses.

Leaders who excel in reliability, those who may lead High Reliability Organizations (HROs), know the Swiss Cheese model (Figure 4.1) and respect that despite defenses, they must accept defenses failing and continually work to reduce the "holes" and minimize the probability of escaping defects. I will cover transformations in product and service quality and use the Swiss Cheese model again. For now, consider it a culture transformation to acknowledge that defenses have holes and that multiple parties need to perform root cause analysis with an open mind to potential errors.

The parties included CR and its design, marketing, sales, and manufacturing, as well as CR's customer, who assembled our component into its larger

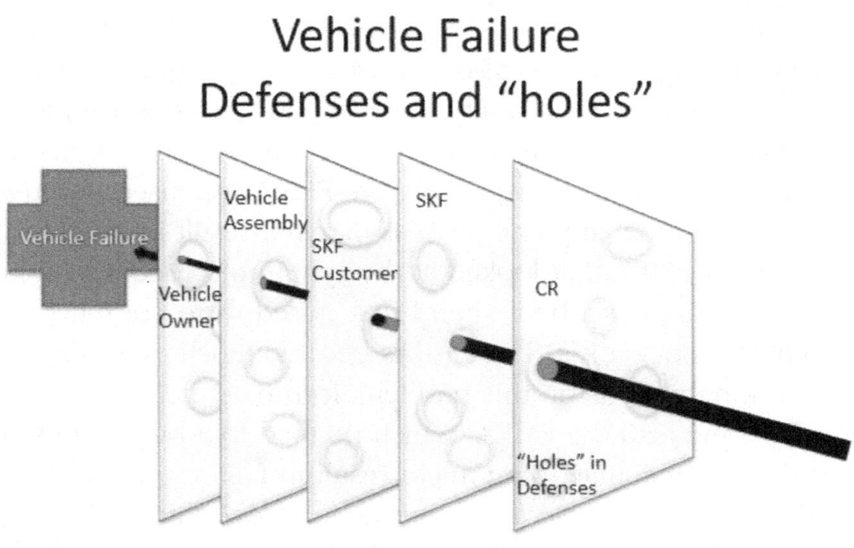

Figure 4.1 Swiss Cheese model of defenses and failure

component. SKF's customer would then assemble the SKF/CR component into a more complex assembly, which would finally be installed onto the vehicle. But the root cause analysis did not stop there because the engineers had experience with maintenance not being performed or maintenance damaging the seal, which resulted in the bearing failure that eventually led to the catastrophic failure.

Leading to excel required CR to accept the Swiss Cheese model's premise and to honestly look at its processes for contributions. It was a rough start and thus the learning for transforming an organization.

I share the details to put in context that it was very easy to blame one of the many organizations that could be the site of the root causes. The absence of Principle 2: Utilize the 3Ms resulted in no data to refute that it was someone else. High Reliability Organizations know the Swiss Cheese Model and are more likely to find multiple root causes than those who "wash their hands" of any responsibility when their inspection suggests no defect. Deming and others showed how parts that meet the specifications may still contribute to failure when the variation still allowed in specifications stacks up; these tolerances of mating parts result in a more complex assembly failing.

This was a cultural shift for some – that their parts meet specification yet the variation in processing might ignore the stack-up of tolerances may result in an assembly failing. The Six Sigma training, Principle 1: Problem-solving skill development, started to change the culture to one more like an HRO. Step one in solving this complex problem began with transforming the culture to be more like an HRO.

Principle 6: Manage risk was also was weak before but strengthened considerably in transforming the Quality organizations at CR and some in SKF and our customer. SKF's customer came to me after we solved this failure, asking for advice on "System FMEA." System FMEA was used because of the Swiss Cheese model that any one process may not result in a failure, so we had to develop an FMEA that looked at the system of processes and organizations. The FMEA's I described when I first joined were not much help to point us to likely root causes. The FMEAs became much more thorough by the teams working with us on this problem, fortunately.

Ernie helped me lead the FMEA, which pointed to a probability that a variable in the seal manufacturing might result in failure. Any seal and bearing will fail over time because it is a mechanical device and one that incurs friction. So, the bearing industry had coached its customers to perform preventive maintenance, including checking the function of the bearing. It took the new variable of vehicle owners thinking they did not have to ever check the bearing to be the "holes lining up" to every result in the vehicle failure.

Utilizing the 3Ms, Ernie measured a variable in the manufacture of the seal, discovered variation, and worked with the floor engineer to set up a statistical process control (SPC) chart to improve the process control of the variable. That was accepted by the facility engineer and the manager, we thought.

I went out to the seal manufacturing process to see if the engineer had reduced the variation the SPC was in place to monitor and prevent escaping bad seals. What I found was a cultural flaw instead. I noticed the frontline assembler of the seal was not plotting the production as Ernie had set up. The operator told me he was told he didn't need to keep plotting. This was a failure of Principle 8: Keep utilizing the 3Ms. The operator told me he was told to stop plotting because nothing was being heard about problems.

I asked the operator if he had seen the variation that resulted in the chart being required, and he said yes. I expected to see the SPC chart showing special cause variation, but what I saw on the chart indicated that the variable hinted the process was very stable. The SPC chart is not intended to plot defects; it is intended to show that the variable was changing in a pattern and thus to stop and investigate before seals failed to meet specifications. SPC is an early warning, but there was nothing on the chart that showed what the operator told me was occurring. The fact that some seals were completely void of a material and thus the SPC chart would have shown this.

When I asked the operator why the data points don't match what he just said, he replied that the engineer told him if he had a seal that was too low in that variable, to not plot it. "Grab another seal" and plot that seal. Principle 1: Problem-Solving Skill and Principle 6L: Risk management failed to be practiced. Principle 5: Engage and Go See saved us because if we had believed the variable was well controlled and thus could not be a root cause of the vehicle failure, we would have misspoken and possibly dismissed the production process that had to be improved. The culture of acceptance and the tendency to not utilize measurement, as well as good risk management that SPC provided, had to change.

Some good news: The operator noticed that when he got a seal that was not of good quality, he noticed the pump that was critical in the assembly sometimes did not work well. This is why Ernie had put the SPC chart out there in the first place. The operator and engineer knew we could not rely on the pump.

The manager agreed to reinstate the SPC charting without biasing the chart by only charting good parts. We thanked the operator for sharing the observation of the pump, and the engineer instructed the operator to now chart all seals including the seals that would highlight potential defects and contribute to a bearing failure that might result in a vehicle failure. Even though the power washing alone done by the customer to its fleet in the field might not cause the vehicle failure, the seal defect and power washing increased the probability.

It took a culture change in the quality organization of the facility to eliminate this root cause. The culture shifted from no news is good news to understanding the Swiss Cheese model teaches that there are holes in every defense and the benefit of SPC to know if the hole allows escaping defects.

Culture and norms that promote that no news is good news resulted in a need for the transformation in quality organizations across CR and the culture. We immediately started discussing in the Six Sigma training that the culture was found to be a root cause, and thus the value in utilizing measuring and managing to the measure made it easier to prevent escaping defects. Eventually, the engineer and operators found it easier to know when the pump was varying. The SPC became proof of their improvements.

We also saw the culture change to stop production instead of "plotting a better part than the one we picked up." This change was huge, and there are books written about how others transformed their quality organizations with the principles of engaging and go see, utilizing the 3Ms, and better risk management.

SKF and Six Sigma in Financial Forecasting

Tom Johnstone was proud of SKF forecasting because it was very accurate. I wanted the algorithm so I could use its success in training forecasting within SKF, but I was told by the forecast team leadership, who Tom pointed me to, that it was proprietary and they were reluctant to share. No problem, I said, I will use other examples of forecasting being done. But for fun, I got the financial forecast data that this forecasting wonder team used.

In my next meeting with Tom and the Executive Officers, I updated them on the Six Sigma training rolling out across SKF and shared how Six Sigma and Minitab can improve forecasting of demand, supply, and other non-financial forecasts, purposely avoiding the appearance of competing with the financial forecasting team who resisted giving me the algorithm.

I had asked Claes prior to the meeting if it was OK to demonstrate the forecasting skill module with the example I describe next. He said, "Go for it." Tom values the truth, and Tom did. You should have seen Tom when I demonstrated, in a few clicks, a forecast that reproduced his wonder team's financial forecast. That little demonstration helped improve the "Quality IQ" of SKF, and I hope it ignited a little humility and even better forecasting from this wonder team for Tom.

Summary

We started the transformation of the Quality Organization at SKF Seals America and then globally with Principle 1: Problem-solving skills and added to the training the fundamentals of understanding variation and better ways to measure it, making it easier to achieve quality. The Quality team shifted when the strategy changed from ISO focus to supporting plants and suppliers with higher reliability practices including Six Sigma's prevention vs. inspection.

Principle 2: Utilize the 3Ms contributed to now measuring using the SKF ZD program, which used the customer's own measure of CR quality. The SPC is a more micro example of utilizing measurement, managing it using SPC, and then making it easier to speak up when things didn't seem right. The Quality organization changed the scoreboard to include ZD outcomes and key process variables that needed process control.

Principle 3: SMART goals again were instrumental by measuring the number of months a production line went without a defect complaint. We also began to measure the facilities by the percentage of production lines achieving the ZD Award.

Principle 4: Competitive Forces matching the organizational structure was proven with the Ferrari F1 customer. Scuderia awarded SKF with 100% of its business. I learned much from Claes and SKF in the science of quality and hopefully helped CR in transforming its culture closer to SKF's. CR transformed its culture and was adding ZD Awards, which allowed marketing and sales to promote seals quality content achievement.

Principle 5: Engage and Go See was a principle Al practiced well before CR when he was at Eaton. He often said he could tell the health of the plant by going out to the receiving and shipping docks and ensuring inventory was flowing well. If stacked up, bad news was coming.

Principle 6: Managing risk was much better executed by using Six Sigma principles and tools like FMEA. Even though CR performed FMEAs before because the Big Three auto manufacturers required them, they were not taken seriously enough, which is why the seal variable was not designed out and not managed on the floor until the transformation.

Principle 7: Celebrate quick wins became the culture with George. No one had better rapport than George with every level in the organization. George was a big promoter of quality and was visible both across CR and at SKF HQ promoting the improvement in culture.

Principle 8: Keep Utilizing the 3Ms was assured with Al running Operations. Al and I had taken the need to measure frequently we practiced at Lincoln and applied it successfully at SKF. Measuring in real time on the shop floor using SPC is but one of many improvements made.

Finally, Silvio Rubatto, SKF Group Director, shared in October 2024 that the ZD Award Program eventually was idled. As we shared in Chapter 1, one should monitor the quality of the measurement system. SKF knew the weakness in measuring complaints accurately and fairly and ensured the measurement system analysis (MSA) was ongoing. The MSA did its job by finding that some were starting to game the measure. Principle 8: Keep utilizing the 3Ms is especially important when the process is not immune to variation. In other words, if the possibility of variation improved to 0%, there would be little need for an MSA to continue, and this is also the case for statistical process control. He acknowledged that some had started to take advantage of the weakness in the measurement system. Silvio was working on utilizing IT vs. the manual complaint reporting before he left SKF.

Notes

1. Source: ISO https://www.iso.org/news/2016/08/Ref2109.html
2. Ford Quality shifts to Six Sigma 6/13/2001 article. Management: Ford Embraces Six Sigma – The New York Times (nytimes.com) Management: Ford Embraces Six Sigma – The New York Times (nytimes.com) https://www.nytimes.com/2001/06/13/business/management-ford-embraces-six-sigma.html
3. Source: https://www.skf.com/us/industries/automotive/cars-and-light-trucks/skf-and-ferrari
4. Source: https://www.qualitychampions.org/curriculum Received permission on 10/22/24 from Dr. Phillips.
5. Reason, James. *Managing the Risks of Organizational Accidents*, Ashgate, Surrey, 1997.

Chapter 5

Transforming Administrative Processes

Finance Examples

I left a great company for a great company. Motorola recruited me to support it globally in quality. I found it surprising that the firm that won the Malcolm Baldrige Award, crediting its Six Sigma for its transformation in quality, was still about getting better. Two GE executives had recently joined Motorola and found an opportunity to utilize Six Sigma more to improve both quality and productivity. Mike Fenger, Motorola's Chief Quality Officer (CQO), and Mike Zafirovski, Chief Operating Officer, when I joined, were building a corporate initiatives group to build on Motorola's Six Sigma and deploy it where improvement was most needed. They both had seen firsthand how GE benefited from Six Sigma and wanted someone who had utilized Six Sigma in productivity gains, not just quality.

Mike Fenger also knew Six Sigma worked far beyond the manufacturing floor when GE applied Six Sigma across its functions. Both Mikes started with Principle 1: Problem-Solving Skills and Principle 4: Competitive force strategy and organizational structure match. Mike recruited me to find out why Motorola's own Six Sigma was not having the impact the Mikes saw at GE. I was also to prepare to deploy support for its businesses leading teams solving Motorola's most severe quality and productivity issues. I asked Mike in my final interview before being hired why he was asking an outsider to fix the Six Sigma program. Mike answered that he found it to be lacking when he joined and he needed the Six Sigma skills to include productivity

DOI: 10.4324/9781032639574-5

as well as quality. My experience in the Eaton and SKF transformations both included quality and productivity improvements, and Motorola was losing market share in a couple of key businesses and may need to transform those units.

In my first week, I found the root cause of Motorola slipping in its capture of value from Six Sigma. The training curricula were not Six Sigma. Mike Fenger asked me to first fix whatever was wrong with Motorola's training because he was confused why Motorola was not talking the talk, and as its CQO, he was finding many problems to solve and thus made the decision to start the Corporate Initiatives Group. Note that he did not name our group the "Transformation" group. Thank goodness because I seldom find a group with transformation in its name that transformed anything. Before Mike joined Motorola, Motorola had a group that was trying to capture some value back to the much-acclaimed Six Sigma, and I heard they were marketing Six Sigma now as new and improved and used the term Digital Six Sigma. The leader of the group had left the company, and Mike Fenger knew he had an issue with leaders knowing the Quality Science, and he sensed Motorola's recently revised Six Sigma training was a contributor. Motorola had put in charge an MBA who had little to zero experience with Six Sigma and operations. I was trained in Six Sigma while at Eaton by former Motorolans, and the internal training looked very little like what I was taught.

Maybe one of the causes of Motorola's internal Six Sigma training was Motorola's regret years later that it did not copyright the name Six Sigma. I heard this when I found out about Motorola's "Digital Six Sigma (DSS)." The training had to change to fit the narrative that Digital Six Sigma was something new and thus would allow copyright ownership. The term and the training supporting Six Sigma were different. It sure was, and I found no evidence the application was working. Thus, I understood Mike's request now to improve Six Sigma and get results. The Director over the training was let go before I arrived, and most of us were new and had no qualms about fixing the training. I wanted to know what DSS was, what made it different from Six Sigma, and in the end, it was marketing fluff.

The curricula had shifted from core quality science practices including statistical process control (SPC), MSA, and skills in problem-solving to what looked like courses I took in my University of Illinois Executive MBA program. I was reading the curricula in my first week to quickly know what Digital Six Sigma was to accurately portray it to the businesses I would support. The training was essentially MBA curricula and did not develop problem-solving skills.

Motorola Finance is the focus of this story and I will reinforce the universality of these principles in Finance and end with a story on Motorola transforming one IT organization while again sharing a manufacturing success and evidence of all eight principles.

Russ Hammer, a Finance Vice President (VP), and I met while supporting Motorola Automotive. Motorola Automotive was struggling in the ultra-competitive auto supplier market. Russ had the vision that Finance, not just Engineering and Manufacturing, could benefit from Six Sigma. Mike Fenger fully supported Finance and every organization within Motorola learning the Quality Science and Six Sigma, and Russ took full advantage of the fact that our Corporate Initiatives Group would support his vision of Finance utilizing Six Sigma for Finance processes.

Let's jump forward a year after joining Motorola and leading a team of Master Black Belts to correct the internal Motorola Six Sigma training. The President of Automotive requested that Mike Fenger include me in MOT Automotive. I was honored but concerned because I heard rumors MOT might spin off its renowned business, the one that made MOT famous. Mike Fenger dismissed the rumor, saying Automotive is critical to Motorola's "Seamless Mobility" vision. MOT was developing technology that we take for granted today, such as starting a cellular phone conversation in the house, walking to the car, and continuing the conversation and traveling long distances without dropping the call. Mike coached me to take the auto role and help MOT where it needed help most. We solved a lot of issues in a short time, and I got to know Russ which was the best thing to happen for me to help MOT corporate-wide.

Russ is a phenomenal leader and mentor to Finance members. He wanted a couple of young Finance members to learn quality improvement by doing. He asked if I would include two very bright Finance team members, and it was a joy. Catherine and Christopher quickly picked up Six Sigma and helped MOT Auto improve operations in MOT's facility in Nogales, Mexico. Russ used their success to convince MOT's Chief Financial Officer (CFO), David Devonshire, to apply Six Sigma to Finance's most vexing issues.

Sarbanes Oxley[1] had become a heavy burden on both Finance and MOT businesses because of an overreaction to placing controls years earlier to meet this new law. This would haunt many organizations, including financial services organizations I will cover later.

Sarbanes-Oxley Act (SOX) Public Law 107–204 – July 30, 2002, is an act to protect investors by improving the accuracy and reliability of corporate disclosures made pursuant to the securities laws, and for other purposes. The financial scandals at Enron, WorldCom, and other large publicly held corporations eroded confidence in the statements made by these organizations, and investors lost billions of dollars when these organizations failed or lost value. The failures also severely negatively impacted the auditing firms who missed the financial misstatements.

MOT and probably every firm affected tried to meet this new law by putting in controls to comply. The law itself is a complex one amounting to 66 pages. Russ and David knew MOT had implemented an excess of controls in haste to meet this new complex law. I joined MOT in 2004 after a couple of years of MOT adding controls, which is a reasonable amount of time for both Finance and every business within MOT to feel the pain of excess controls.

Fenger had recruited me to improve Six Sigma's value in improving productivity having already proven Six Sigma's value in improving quality across the globe since MOT invented Six Sigma. This seemed a great test case for MOT to apply Six Sigma to both productivity problems and in Finance.

Russ Hammer and Ed Hughes, both VPs of Finance, with Russ in charge of internal auditing and controls and supporting businesses, recruited me to join MOT Finance. I was delighted to join Finance for three reasons: 1. I could make a bigger impact across MOT compared to just supporting Automotive. 2. I still believed MOT would sell off Auto. 3. My leader in MOT Automotive was notorious for poor behaviors not supported by Motorola.

A Ninth Principle?

This was the second time in my 25 years of working that I discovered a poor leader can never achieve excellence. I found a 100% correlation that poor leaders do not achieve positive transformation. Fortunately, I have only a small sample of poor leadership. I could add a ninth principle that is found in every transformation: quality of leadership, but readers already know that. This leader also had no use for Quality Science nor Six Sigma, and it amazed me how he lasted as long as he did.

A few months after leaving automotive for finance, MOT announced the sale of its storied automotive business to Continental AG. I heard that Continental and this corrosive person soon split after the sale. I was delighted that the plant manager, whom this leader would embarrass in public, went on to lead a major business in a major automotive supplier.

Russ sponsored a team of MOT Finance managers from across the globe to apply Six Sigma to eliminate useless or redundant controls. Mary Pat Bitter led her peers in problem-solving and they made a significant reduction in controls while improving SOX compliance. Mary Pat continues to excel as a leader and is the CFO for MOT Lenovo.

The team would meet around a large map of the controls and apply rules to judge the controls. These controls impacted not just Finance but many in operations that had to either collect data or spend time on actions that added no value to MOT's customers. I coached the team Value-Stream Mapping, a popular tool created by the authors Rother and Shook, who developed a mapping routine with icons that are easy to use in learning to see waste. Their book, Learning to See[2], was a popular book in many companies I later consulted and is now a part of the best Six Sigma training courses.

Mike Fenger continued to capitalize on successes from his team in the Corporate Initiatives Group. Mike was one of the brightest leaders I worked for who went on to lead Apple iPhone Sales for Steve Jobs. Mike knew he had to develop leaders in MOT, and as CQO led the development of MOT's Quality Vital Signs (QVS) Program. His work is of much value in this book because he targeted leaders. His experience learning from Jack Welch at GE was that leadership is key to success in complex organizations.

Mike identified that leaders were exempt from the quality sciences in many MOT businesses and had not capitalized on MOT's Six Sigma. Mike lived Principle 1: Problem-Solving Skill Development and, unsurprisingly, targeted every MOT leader to build skills.

His QVS Program and skill development were required of every leader, and our Corporate Initiatives Group teamed with Motorola University for its infrastructure, providing training to develop, and deliver the training worldwide.

The QVS listed six quality essentials Mike believed necessary for the Quality Turnaround he and Mike Zafirovski determined necessary. These essentials were:

1. Business, Finance, and Services
2. New Product Introduction Software
3. New Product Introduction Hardware
4. Manufacturing

5. Sourcing
6. Executing a Quality Turnaround

I supported MOT University in most of its training with Six Sigma concepts pulled from MOT's original training as well as the refreshed training our team implemented, replacing the MBA-like curricula that contributed to MOT losing its Six Sigma improvement rate.

I led the development of several modules for the first Essentials: Business, Finance, and Services, having worked in my first year with its business and finance. Mike built the QVS Program to initially change the culture – to improve the Quality IQ, which had been weakened over time. These six essentials were the specific focus areas considered most important in Motorola's Quality Turnaround.

I took Mike's lead and helped develop the electives for leaders in Finance. Readers would do well to copy these essentials and thus cover them in some detail for better understanding.

The electives included those skills David, Russ, and Ed Hughes valued most in quality and Six Sigma and would give Finance the most improvement. The electives beyond the required course in Digital Six Sigma Overview for Leaders were:

- Learn from Quality Leaders, where I taught the works of Deming, Juran, Crosby, Ishikawa, and Shingo, and related to MOT Finance and its businesses
- Quality's Four Critical Success Factors (CSF). Based on my experience at Eaton and SKF, the four CSFs great leaders nailed were leadership commitment, choosing the right projects, choosing the right people for skills but skills for all, and building the infrastructure to support a transformation
- DSS and Productivity Skills. The Value-Stream Mapping module taught us how to see waste as Roher and Shook indicated, which is vital to taking waste out and I used examples of successes we achieved in MOT Automotive and MOT Finance. We also learned from the successes of Motorola
- Risk Management, Principle 6: Manage Risk was much needed, as we learned in my first project in the OnStar failure. Thanks again to Bill Cooper whose success is covered later in this chapter. Bill and the team proved MOT's services could also benefit, specifically IT and Finance with their SOX controls improvement utilizing Failure Mode and Effects

Analysis (FMEA) in deciding controls to reduce or eliminate risks that did not warrant

- Forecasting and SPC Overview was another elective and vital to Finance. I learned from David Devonshire, CFO at MOT, that Finance is measured by its forecast quality. He coached his business Finance leaders that making the forecast, or in other words, achieving the outcome you predicted, is the Quality Vital Sigma for forecasting. He added that beating your forecast is a variation that should not be celebrated. Investment decisions could be wrong based on forecasts. Beating a forecast suggests that the business did not know its variables well enough and could cause concern among investors. In a publicly held company, this can cause negative impacts.

These modules were partially developed using what I helped SKF discover. I also borrowed the Zero defects program elements including SMART goals from SKF. In critical outcomes such as "making your numbers," an organization can achieve zero defects, at least for a time, and should strive for nothing less.

At this time in business, there was a lot of pushback against striving for zero defects because many thought zero was impossible, especially with the popularity of SMART goal preaching. In healthcare, I will cover Zero Defects rang true even more when patient safety and preventable mortality became unacceptable. Zero defects were possible, and nothing less should be in a SMART goal when catastrophic failure is possible.

I started delivering the training to MOT leadership through the frontline administrative service teammates worldwide. Motorola had facilities in some of the most beautiful areas of the world, and meeting Motorola folks and living in their cultures is still a career highlight. These sites included Europe, Asia, South America, and across North America. I taught all levels of Finance, and while in the country, I was also teaching the other services and manufacturing businesses, thus getting to know MOT very well.

Motorola was a tremendous company and market leader in many of its products. Sadly, today it is a much smaller company, having sold semiconductor business before I joined, as well as its cellular communications group and automotive division. It was clear that Principle 4: Competitive force strategy and organizational structure was becoming more important in the cellular products business, which eventually sold off after losing its market share dominance to competitors. Not surprisingly, I found that the technology Motorola developed was now led by leaders who had not utilized Six

Sigma. I sensed the leaders thought their business was too cool and different from the pager business, where MOT had earned the highest market share by far but was losing it to competitors and new entrants. As Porter's Five Forces concept explains, the forces that affect outcomes must be strategically considered.

Regulatory forces are included in Porter's Competitive Five Forces. AT&T and Motorola developed the cellular network[3] and the handset, but later the Federal Communications Commission (FCC) forced each to choose one or the other. This regulatory force, whether good or bad or both, is a force that can affect a single organization's ability to transform outcomes for consumers. I have experienced regulatory impacts on the degree of transformation in electrical power distribution, and now cellular communications, and we will see this force again in healthcare and financial services. Porter's Five Forces is a powerful concept to maximize outcomes by identifying the forces and adjusting early on. What Eaton could have done with Industrial Breaker by not forcing the sale to a very small inexperienced competitor will never be known. I know firsthand the success we had in improving its quality and margins that were then stopped due to selling the Industrial Breaker. The Feds requiring us to sell may well have had the opposite effect if the buyer failed to maintain the market share we earned.

Motorola and Principle 4: Competitive Force Strategy in Cellular Communications. The history of Motorola shows many examples of strategic thinking. After all, Motorola and AT&T are considered by many to have developed the cellular communication business. From Motorola's website:

> **Cellular Innovations Highlights**
>
> Motorola's website covers the highlights from its development of Cellular
>
> ***September 21, 1983***
> *After 10 years and more than a US$100 million investment, Motorola received type acceptance for the world's first portable cellular phone system and world's first handheld cell phone, the DynaTAC 8000X.*

Once again, we see how regulators can affect transformation and business. Federal regulation entered into cellular communications early on, prohibiting AT&T and Motorola from owning both the cellular infrastructure and handsets. We will never know what Motorola could have achieved if it had been able to develop these two key components of cellular. Regardless, it sold the business after losing market share dominance, and the learning for transformations is to recognize the forces at play and strategize to address and leverage them or cease to exist.

Regardless of the regulatory impact, Motorola Cellular was going down a different path than First Responder Radios, which exists today.

I attended an internal conference at MOT's cellular business to hear a very popular author who had written on excellence. I was surprised that the speaker spoke of Six Sigma as more of a burden to innovation and said that this business should ignore it and just do it. Not surprisingly, this business had the lowest Quality IQ of any business within MOT, and it was too proud, I guess, to utilize Mike's program initially. Mike was eventually asked to focus on the Cellular business, but it was too late. Today, the business unit that helped pioneer Six Sigma and MOT's quality, its First Responder Radio business, is MOT today.

Transforming the Quality IQ in IT

In my first week, I was reading the training material and honestly bored. While reading, I overheard my colleague, Jill, on the phone with the President of Motorola Automotive. Motorola started in the automotive industry by developing a radio that would work in the budding auto industry. This business and its President were important to Motorola, even at the time when Motorola co-led the development of cellular communications with AT&T.

Jill was saying to the president that our group did not have the resources to help him solve a big issue with GM because we were just starting. I asked Jill if I could listen in to understand this issue. She said sure, and I heard the president ask for a Black Belt because GM was having Zero Kilometer failures at their vehicle assembly plants. Imagine a huge customer like GM not being able to ship because of your product. The failure was in the telematics unit Motorola developed, and virtually everyone knew it as OnStar. OnStar was failing before the vehicle left the assembly line.

I asked Jill to mute the line and I asked her if I could volunteer to help solve it. She said to me that she heard I wanted out of the automotive industry, to which I remarked I wanted something new but also wanted to help. I also remarked that after reading the training decks, it was pretty clear that

I had to make a change. However, that was not going to be as important as getting OnStar to work.

Jill introduced me to the president, and I volunteered to help. He asked me when I could be at the manufacturing plant in Seguin. I said I could leave that night, and he said great. I just had one question, "Where is Seguin?" He laughed and said near San Antonio, TX.

This chapter is about transforming Finance in a large organization, but once again, we see manufacturing practices are so common that these eight principles were found again in the eventual solving of the OnStar issue. To move on to Finance, I quickly recap how the principles were used to solve the manufacturing/design root causes.

Motorola Quality and Finance Transformation Summary

Transforming organizations within Motorola included IT in one facility and the corporate Finance group in regulatory compliance. Humbly, this great company has transformed itself through the years, becoming the developer of technologies that helped win world wars, reach the moon, and improve how each of us communicates daily. So, these transformations mentioned are minor in comparison. The principles are present and, when absent, thwart significant outcome improvement.

Transformations can be impacted by regulatory forces, as we have seen in the Eaton and Motorola stories. Leadership is wise to address the risk early on and direct the regulation rather than react to it.

Following are the Principles in Summary to Achieve Excellence and Transformational Improvements in Motorola's Financial, IT, and Quality Organizations

Principle 1: Problem-solving skills. Fenger recruited me to improve Motorola's skills because he saw the gap. My first week proved the gap with the OnStar failure. The training in Motorola's own Six Sigma was renewed from an interim confusing focus on business skills from an MBA-like curriculum.

Principle 2: Utilize Measure, Manage to the measure, and Making it easier (3Ms). Automotive had been utilizing 3Ms as any automobile supplier has to by being measured relentlessly by the Big Three, but IT had not utilized measurement of its own contribution to the manufacturing process. We started measuring defects on the production line of OnStar and found where the failure started and eventually fed the test results to the front of the line where the root cause was – solder paste application. Solder paste application is the farthest process step from when a quality failure was known – the final test. So, Bill Cooper, IT Black Belt, helped the team by placing a monitor of real-time test results at the solder paste area. Just this utilization of measure visibility allowed the team to better manage quality and problem-solve. The team found variation in the solder paste application and eventually eliminated many of the failures. Bill made it easier for the team to see the problem and thus easier to solve the problem. Most remarkable in this Motorola story is the transformation of the IT department's role in quality.

IT was also exempt in performing risk management when IT's services were a part of the production process. Neither Motorola nor any of the Big Three noticed that IT was a vital "component" of manufacturing when it supplied the data unique to each OnStar device, just like a fastener was a component of an engine. Yet, IT was never a part of the FMEA, and thus another root cause found was that the wrong data was loaded into the OnStar device in the process. The team also caught this by being able to measure and then manage the test failure measure, which made it easier to ensure the right data was loaded into the right OnStar device.

SKF also contributed to Motorola in this quality turnaround. SKF has been a leader in reliable bearings in its 100 years. Another program in quality besides its Zero Defects was its "Scrap Without Compromise" discipline. SKF found that a source of defects can be created when scrapping production or sometimes just pausing a production line to take a product off the line and inspect it. Putting the product back on the production line sometimes introduced variation causing a new defect. Think of a sushi restaurant conveyor belt again where diners pick dishes from the conveyor. Let's say one diner takes a dish and then decides to put the dish back on the belt. But the diner down the line finds the dish was too salty and we find the earlier diner had salted it, not thinking if it had placed it back on the belt. The restaurant, to achieve better reliability, might consider SWOC and coach diners to NOT put the dish back in the process.

Motorola IT discovered the production team had often taken OnStar devices off the product line to inspect them and mistakenly returned the devices into the wrong carriers on the belt. When it came time for the IT data to be input, the wrong device received the data because it was placed in the wrong carrier.

IT and the production team found that a device may have been taken off the product line and that it created the wrong device in the Data Install step. Again, we dispel the excuse that every industry, every firm, every product, every… is different. These principles, as well as so many other fixes, work across so many organizations.

Principle 3: SMART with radical goals. Mike Fenger was well-versed in the 3Ms and he challenged every leader to take training in quality and achieve a high level of training. It was radical even in Motorola for leaders to strive for Six Sigma Green Belt or Black Belt training until Mike joined.

Principle 4: Competitive force strategy and organizational structure match. The world knows how well GE competed, and Jack Welch made it known that businesses should be #1 or #2 in their markets. Mike wanted Motorola to compete again on quality as it did years earlier when it won the Malcolm Baldrige Award the first time with Six Sigma as a major contributor.

Principle 5: Engage – Go see. Bill and I never would have found the solder paste defect nor the IT data error without seeing it firsthand.

Principle 6: Manage risk. IT now, for the first time at Motorola and probably now a standard with GM with other suppliers, utilized FMEA to improve reliability when IT was instrumental to production quality.

Principle 7: Celebrate quick wins. I found my favorite BBQ ribs when the Motorola CQO hosted the Seguin team celebrating the GM executives rewarding Motorola for solving the OnStar issues. It was on this trip that GM's executive highlighted that ISO did not prevent the failure; it was Motorola's Six Sigma that solved the Zero Kilometer Failures.

Principle 8: Keep utilizing the 3Ms. Bill Cooper shared that the Seguin plant continued to help operators see in real time the measure of quality. He also scrolled and replicated the use of risk management in many more IT processes.

Lastly – A principle to never do: Attempt change without considering the principles.

Transformations show evidence of every principle. The sequence may differ as leaders learn the principles and opportunities arise.

Transforming Financial Services with The Scientific Approach to Achieve Excellence

Tackling conflicting priorities is a must. Recognizing them requires an astute person and a scientific approach. The scientific approach is to find truth and then verify by working to disprove the hypothesis. Too much emphasis on achieving the goal without a scientific approach may result in believing a transformation occurred, only to find future results disprove anything special happened. Using the scientific approach minimizes the bias called confirmation bias. This bias is the tendency to interpret results and information in a way that confirms or supports one's wishes or believed.

This story shows how a transformation was achieved, but first we needed a better scientific approach in the key performance indicator to be used to declare success. The charts I was shown in my first days of joining this team and the interpretation from leaders of those charts hinted that what they thought might not be the truth.

This story can fit any organization and is about paying its customers what is owed them. Warranty reimbursement is an example of a firm needing to pay what it owes based on its contract with the customer. Any transaction that reimburses a customer can take this approach I am about to show you and apply it. Once applied, the credibility of transformative outcomes is much higher and, more importantly, team members can trust the key measure along the journey as they work to improve it.

I use an example of a firm that reimburses its customers for repairs needed after an accident. The leaders of the organization received a line chart showing the accuracy in the amount paid that should have been paid every quarter from the data analytics team. The chart also had a few quarters of history to compare and look for trends. The leaders would interpret almost any change quarter to quarter as a sign that something changed in accuracy.

The Key Performance Indicator Chart Originally Used

I asked the leaders what the goal in accuracy was and was told they wanted 92% accuracy. The combination bar and line chart the leaders were given did not show the goal, and this was an opportunity missed and quickly corrected [See Figure 5.1]. One had no idea what "good" is. With a goal line we will add later, everyone who sees the chart knows the performance relative to the goal. But that was not my major concern.

Perfect accuracy translated means that if paid perfectly, this chart would show a line at 100%. A 92% translates that the actual pay was 8% incorrect, whether paid too much or too little. Accuracy is measured in US dollars, so 8% meant 8% of the total amount of dollars paid was inaccurate. When leadership states a goal, they should be crystal clear to all about what the goal means, and it starts with how it is calculated.

I did not know if leadership wanted to have zero payouts below 92% accuracy, or it was OK for the quarter to average 92%. The latter allows 50% of the payouts to be below 92% if 50% are above. Two entirely different understandings.

Leadership landed on a goal for the month to be 92% or better. Note that the chart did not have this goal stated, and I found many did not know what the goal was. Fewer knew what accuracy meant.

On my first day consulting with this organization, leadership was celebrating last quarter's report on one of its two key performance indicators (KPI): Accuracy of paying what we should pay.

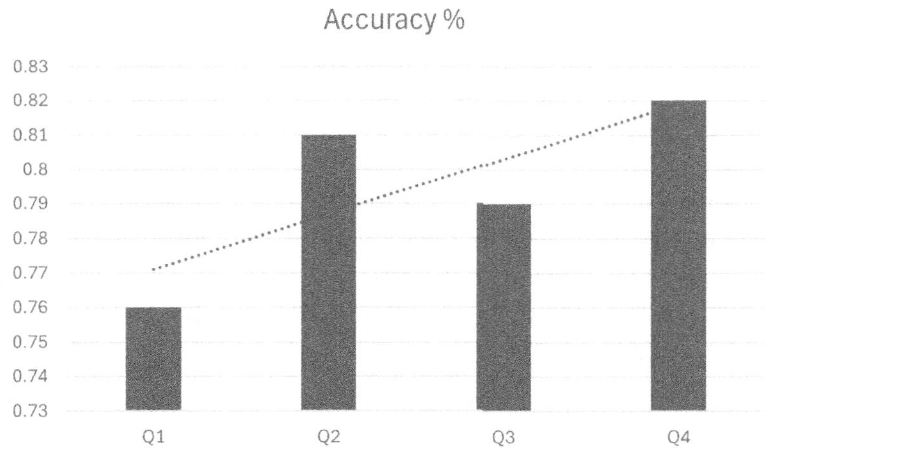

Figure 5.1 Accuracy %.

Original Chart

There are hundreds of payout transactions daily. A transaction is the payment amount to the customer after an event occurred. A frontline employee judges what the company owes based on the event and company policy.

The data for the chart comes from a sampling by another department after payment is made to a customer. The "audit" department judges the amount that should have been paid to the customer using the documentation shared by the original employee judging what is owed. The absolute value of the difference between what was paid and what should have been paid is the ratio, and this ratio is a sum of the audit results over the quarter. This ratio was reported as a percentage.

The third group involved in the charting is the analysis team. It started work in reporting after the quarter ended, and it took them a week or more to report the performance accurately. Therefore, inaccuracies may have occurred four or more months before leadership received the chart and report. There were no other reports available to the frontline, except when the audit department reported a transaction it had questions about.

Leaders who excel understand data, analysis, how best to graphically present, and most of all, how to share performance most honestly with their organizations.

Here are questions I had as I got to know the business. I invite you to look at your KPIs. Every transformation, in my experience starts here ensuring the right KPIs and better analysis to know the truth, and then to drive better outcomes.

To start, what do you think of the span of time leadership that sees the accuracy report? Any questions about the trendline? I see trend lines often on Excel charts, probably because Excel makes it easy to add a trendline. My first question is whether the readers know how the trendline is calculated. They virtually never know but all believe the trend exists if the line goes up or down. This is exactly what leadership believed after seeing this chart. It helps, too, when the trendline is going in the direction leadership wants. I cover this trendline later with this same data to validate if a trend existed.

Another question about the performance indicator is whether a % or ratio is better than the actual dollars paid vs. dollars that should have been paid. How does a percentage add to or detract from the reader's perception of the magnitude of inaccuracy?

My first step in consulting is to know the people and know the business. Knowing the business starts with its key measures of outcome. I was given this chart, the goal, and went to work with my team.

Key Performance Indicator Chart Using Statistical Process Control

We took the chart to my desk and entered the data into Minitab, a statistical software package used by many worldwide. We wanted to see the data with a minimum of bias and to start understanding if there is truly a trend. I used an SPC Chart, which Dr. Shewhart created in the 1920s for this same purpose of knowing if a trend exists or any other sign that the process is changing. Dr. Shewhart helped us understand if trends or anything "special" was occurring [See Figure 5.2].

I spell out some of the acronyms, but otherwise the chart would look just like the one below. Dr. Shewhart, creator of a line chart with some unique and powerful additions to a simple line chart, taught that true change can be better identified. Shewhart differentiated common cause variation from something special, let's say, new variation. Common cause variation exists in the system and will continue to result in an expected and predictable amount of variation. Special cause variation is different. It is a change in the performance not expected, and thus indicative that something new happened.

This technique in graphically displaying performance is the answer for every leader wanting to know if performance is on the path to excel. This technique will verify if a transformation is on its way, and best of all, it gives feedback throughout the transformation journey to everyone – not just leaders once a quarter. I covered SPC in my prior books, utilizing the 3Ms of Process Improvement (and the Healthcare version), as well as in, "Leading High Reliability Organizations in Healthcare," for those wanting to know how to apply SPC today. I focus in this book on how those leading to excel can best utilize SPC to achieve excellence and transformative change.

Chart Using Statistical Process Control Chart Method

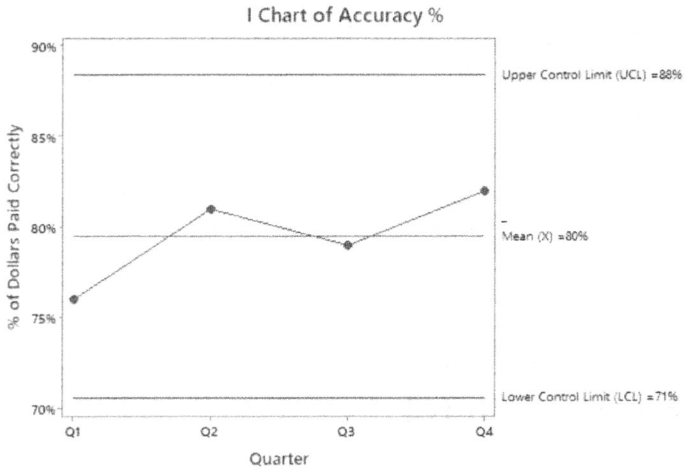

Figure 5.2 Accuracy using SPC.

Statistical process control may add a central tendency line. See the green line labeled as "Mean Accuracy x = 79%." The mean (average) accuracy of the four quarters in this representation is 79%.

Statistical process control will also add one or two control limits. These control limit lines are very valuable and help us interpret if something special occurred. The upper control limit is calculated using all the data available which were four periods. The control limit estimates the uppermost accuracy expected if accuracy had only common cause variation. The lower control limit allows us to see what the lowest (worst) accuracy might be if the process stays operating the same, i.e., nothing special happened.

Statistical process control also provides powerful analysis to determine if trends occur. The control limits and the mean line are key to knowing if a trend occurs. There are tests to know if something special may have occurred [See Figure 5.3]. Using Minitab, test 1 is the first test listed at the top. The remaining tests are sequentially numbered going down the list. Minitab applies the test to the data and will mark the data point red and apply the number of the test when the test first fails. Any test failing demonstrates special cause variation has occurred. The process is "out of control," which also means it has become unstable. Test 1 will fail if the data point is above or below either of the control limits.

The control limits show the boundary of the outcome expected if no special causes occur. This boundary suggests that over 98% of the time, the data is expected to fall within the control limits. The reality of this story is that they had very few data points, and the precision of SPC is limited, as in any statistical test, with so few data points. But there is no reason not to start SPC as soon as one gets two data points. For more information on how much data is required, refer to Minitab or other sources of information on SPC.

In Figure 4.2, there are no red points and no tests noted that failed. Therefore, accuracy is considered stable. Stable also means there are no statistically significant trends. Using SPC to forecast, this organization's accuracy performance is improbable above 88%. If the quarter's accuracy was 90%, we interpret this to mean something special probably happened. In this example, something good happened that had not occurred before. If no data points exceed the control limit (ignoring other tests of control), we conclude only common cause variation is occurring, and insufficient evidence exists to say there is anything special occurring or a trend using the interpretation leadership had made when looking at the chart they saw.

Conclusion: Insufficient evidence of a trend in this data. The leadership should have no confidence that Q4 is showing accuracy has had a shift in performance, because there is no indication that anything special occurred. In addition, leadership should not expect that there is a trend and that accuracy will remain varying around the mean. Leadership was about to celebrate, so I coached them to hold the celebration until more evidence which we were preparing to provide.

Test 2 is a very helpful test and is an example of the extra power of SPC to help identify if a trend or special cause exists. The trend line in Excel is a rolling average, and one has no idea of the level of statistical significance that gives a trend line a slope. Any two points, if not exactly the same, will have a slope. A slope may indicate that special cause variation exists. There is no way to know that by seeing a slope in this calculation of a trend line.

Surprising to many is that there are multiple tests of stability. Data does not have to fall above or below the control limits to see if a special cause or trend exists. Test 2, for example, looks if three data points, quarters in this story, in a row are on the same side of the mean. The mean line is calculated as the average of the four data points. Thus, data points will fall above and below the mean line with about 50% of the dots above the mean when the process is stable.

Conclusion: Insufficient evidence of a trend in this data. There are not even two data points in a row on the same side of the mean.

Test 3: This tests if enough consecutive data points are increasing or decreasing – a trend. Based on the confidence you want, Minitab defaults to requiring 6 points in a row. In other words, we need at least six quarters of data for this test. The trend line test.

Conclusion: Insufficient evidence of a trend in this data. There are not even two data points in a row increasing or decreasing. Leaders now know the value of SPC and how to interpret it. They also realized, having seen no test fail the tests of stability, that performance in the last quarter suggests nothing better or worse is happening with accuracy.

Chart of Tests for Out of Control Conditions

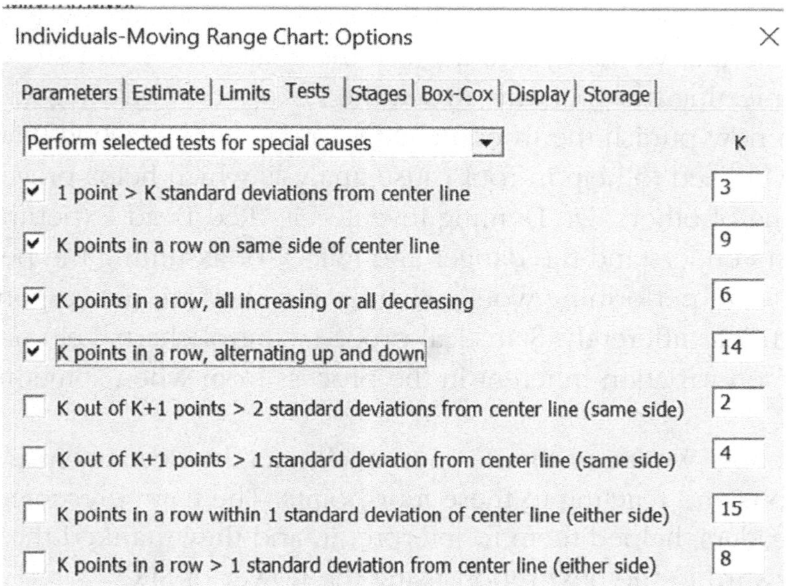

Figure 5.3 SPC tests of control. Source: Minitab.

Statistical Process Control Chart with Goal Line

This is the same chart (Figure 5.4) with the addition of a goal. Let's say leadership wants the minimum goal to be 92% accurate. Adding this line helps us understand performance compared to the goal.

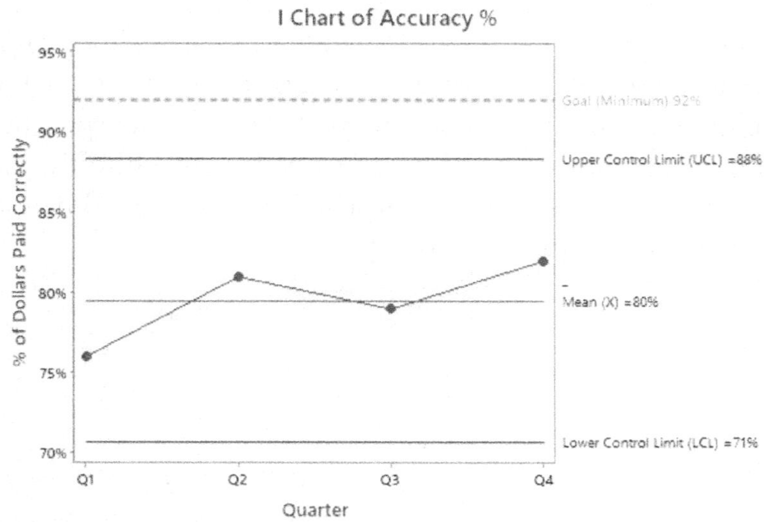

Figure 5.4 Accuracy with goal.

It is acceptable to add goal lines, and quite helpful for the frontline and leadership, with the caveat that one might misinterpret a control limit to be the goal. We see not only that the last quarter's performance was still not at goal but also that we had yet to achieve the goal. Too often I see celebration after meeting the goal only to see the next period below goal. So, does leadership now punish the frontline? NO! Dr. Deming coached that SPC should be utilized to help in root cause analysis which helps prevent erroneous blaming of others. Dr. Deming invented is "Red Bead Experiment" to help leaders understand the danger and fallacy of assuming the people in the process are performing worse when in fact they are not responsible for doing anything differently. Statistical process control charts help us differentiate common variation inherent in the process from when something special occurred.

Interpreting: We know there is not much data, but leadership was making decisions and reacting to these four points. The team presented the SPC Chart to leaders, helped them to interpret it, and they thanked the team and looked forward to the next report using the power of SPC.

Statistical Process Control After Q5

When I joined the team, the analysts had just sent the Q4 report – nearly two months after Q4 ended. Fortunately, Q4 had already finished and the analysts shared their same style of bar chart sooner now that there was even more attention to this KPI. Below is the team's SPC updated with Q5. [See Figure 5.5]

Interpretation: Thankfully the leaders did not buy pizza for improving accuracy because the very next data point showed accuracy back down. The team was thanked by the leaders for the better way of interpreting accuracy data. The SPC Chart showed a stable accuracy rate, much to the chagrin of everyone. But the frontline was not surprised because they knew nothing significant changed to improve accuracy.

Statistical Process Control Chart with Q5

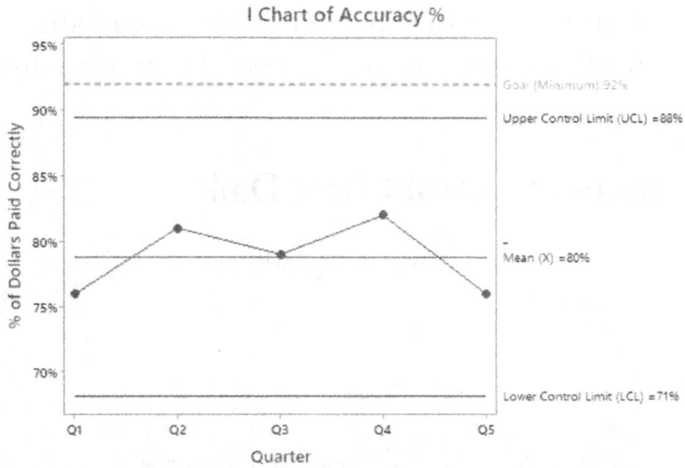

Figure 5.5 Next quarter.

Q5 accuracy went down and SPC tests suggest nothing special by not flagging the Q5 data point.

Charts Support Calls to Action

You know enough now to take any KPI in your organization and use SPC. Take your most important measures and plot them on SPC as we did. Consult with your Black Belt or Quality Engineer about how to correctly use SPC. An Individual SPC Chart is the type of SPC Chart we used here. It may also be called an X chart. This chart is usually good enough and results in a correct interpretation for continuous data and even some attribute data. Again, talk to your Black Belt or Quality Engineer or a course on SPC. Minitab is very helpful with its ease of use and tutorials included.

Improving the Scoreboard

The organization not only had to wait weeks to know what the prior quarter's accuracy was, but it also only saw four data points a year. By the time leadership saw the accuracy, months may have passed. Root cause analysis is much more difficult so late after the process happened. Increasing the frequency of posting of the score can often make a tremendous improvement.

There is a saying when using charts that are far in the past, "It's like driving looking in the rear-view mirror."

The team took all the data they had and instead of plotting the mean for each quarter, they plotted each day's mean on SPC. [See Figure 5.6]

Statistical Process Control Chart Daily

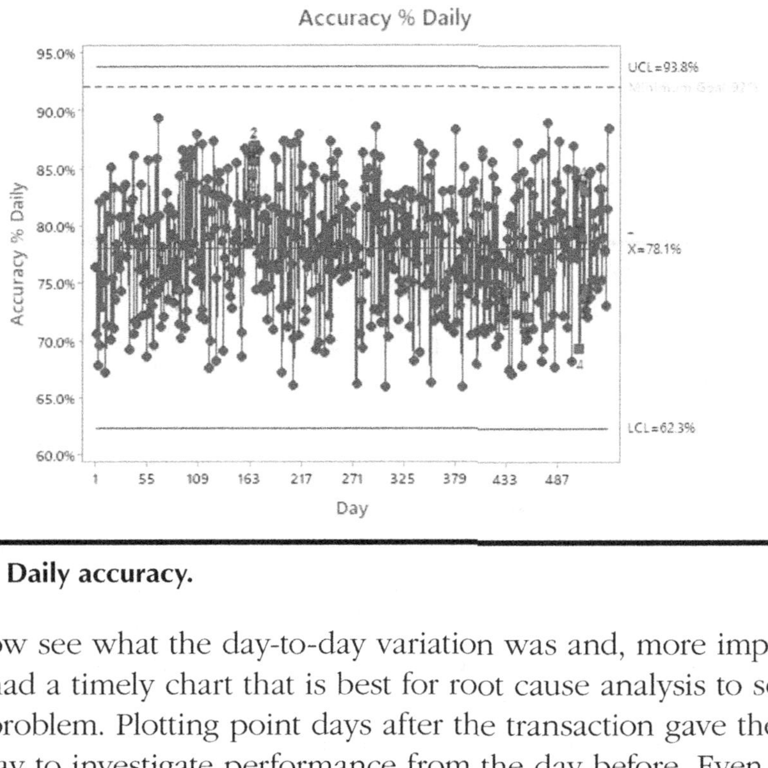

Figure 5.6 Daily accuracy.

We can now see what the day-to-day variation was and, more importantly, the team had a timely chart that is best for root cause analysis to solve the accuracy problem. Plotting point days after the transaction gave the frontline a better way to investigate performance from the day before. Even getting this chart a few days later allowed team members to remember what might have happened that resulted in the accuracy score. Principle 1: Developing problem-solving skills should include the value in frequent and timely reporting.

The team did well not only getting the data daily but they also in obtaining it within days of the transaction, resulting in paying the customer. This necessitated speeding up the audit department's process to judge accuracy, too. Great things often happen by simply speeding up the knowledge of performance. We started seeing improvement nearly immediately after sharing the daily chart with the frontline and QA.

We also found variation in the audit department's judgment. The measurement system itself was affecting the accuracy percentage performance. The audit department began contacting the frontline, and it was now easier for both the frontline and the audit to discover what went wrong the day or two before when they saw a significant change in the daily chart. This is like the conductor of an orchestra directing the entire orchestra based only on the horn section. Or imagine a baseball team not changing pitchers because no one reports the score until three months after the ball game ended. Problem-solving is so much better, faster, and easier when data is presented quickly.

The team started plotting daily and created a daily problem-solving cadence. Look what happened after adding the data from the prior chart. In the first days of problem-solving, the SPC Chart using Minitab started showing tests failing and thus evidence that the improvements the team was making were creating special cause variation – improvement! [See Figure 5.7]

Statistical Process Control Chart after Team Problem-Solving Began

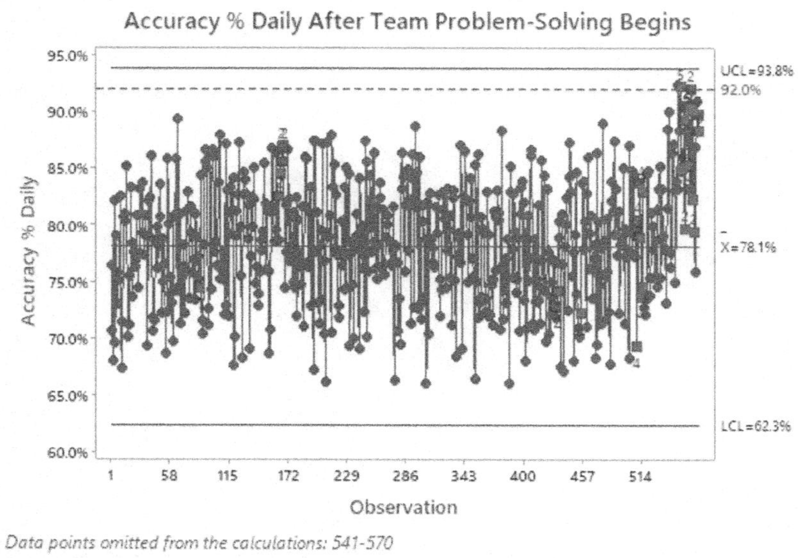

Figure 5.7 Daily after improvement started.

The frontline and leadership now saw the performance on a daily basis, and the "Out of control" performances were noted by each data point on the chart, accompanied by a number referring to the test in Minitab shown earlier. An example is the data point marked with a 2. This means that day showed a special cause variation of nine points (9 consecutive days) in which the mean daily was on the same side of the center line. It is improbable that the team could have achieved 9 days in a row above the average historically. This, therefore, is a sign of special cause variation. Something changed in the process, allowing improvement to occur.

The team members working in the process felt great. And they wanted a chart they could use every day. The team came up with this simpler chart with enough history to see the most recent day's performance in context. [See Figure 5.8]. This chart used the prior month's accuracy performance and a vertical reference line ending at month six to note when the team began problem-solving in month 7.

Statistical Process Control Chart Shared with Frontline and Quality Every Day

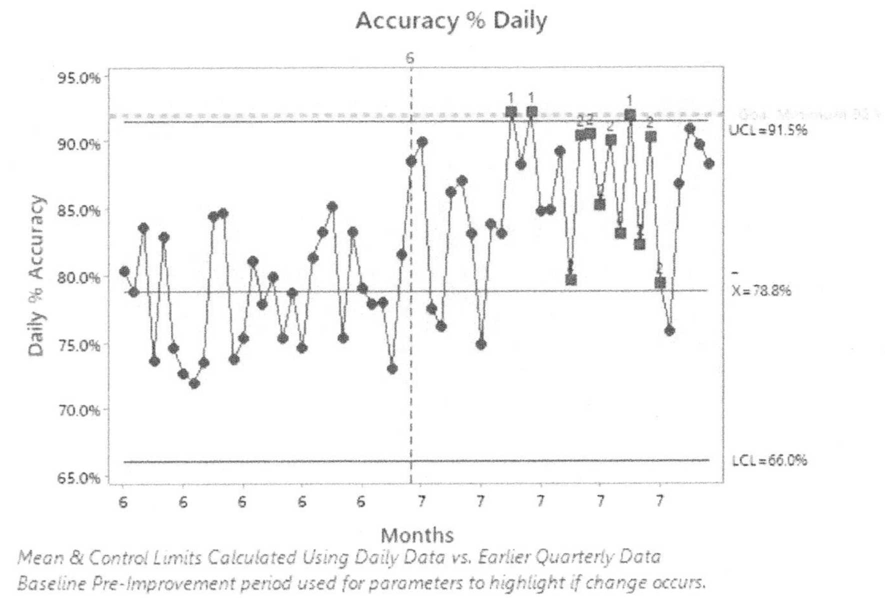

Figure 5.8 Daily scoreboard chart.

The control limits and means were calculated using this same data. Slight changes in these parameters can be explained by taking slightly different data to start the chart. The baseline was unfortunately stable, meaning accuracy was not improving, but this stability gave them more confidence that future improvements were occurring using the tests in SPC. It is good practice to use the baseline period to calculate the mean and control limits, also known as parameters. This allows for the comparison of future data against the baseline. Statistical process control can recalculate the parameters with each addition of data, or one can compare new data against the original parameters. This chart is an SPC Chart of the baseline period with its calculated control limits and mean. It was easy to compare data after improvement efforts began by continuing to use these baseline calculated parameters with the daily data coming in once improvement efforts began. We call this "Locking in" parameters for a before and after fair comparison.

Good news! Test 1 failed. The daily mean exceeded the upper control limit. This was a big day for the team, giving high confidence that accuracy was finally improving. Test 2 failing was further evidence that improvement was occurring because it tests if 9 or more days had a mean higher than the past.

Statistical Process Control Method to Confirm Improvement

Statistical process control once again provides a way to know if improvement is occurring. Once the SPC Chart is created and SPC tests confirm that special cause variation has occurred and this change in performance is continuing, SPC can be helpful in seeing this new level of performance. The feature in Minitab is called "Stage." [See Figure 5.9]

Statistical Process Control Chart Using Stages to Compare Before and After Improvement Efforts Begin

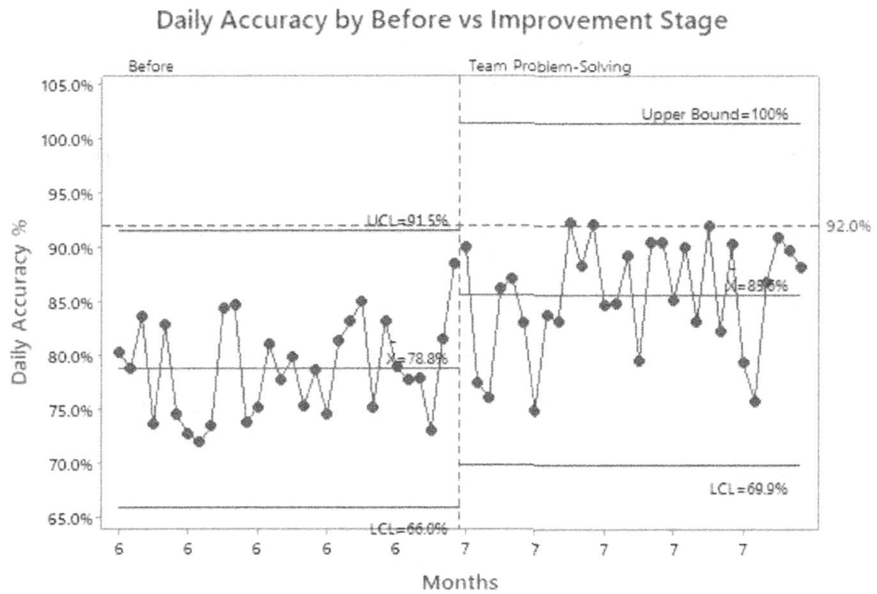

Figure 5.9 Before and after improvement.

Caution: Do not use stages unless the SPC using baseline parameters has proven something changed – special cause variation occurred. This method I share will almost always show a different mean and control limits, but one does not know if these changes are statistically significant. The SPC tests give us this confidence of statistically significant change.

This SPC Chart has two sections – before and after the team started improvement efforts. The prior SPC Chart proved change was occurring because daily accuracy exceeded the previously calculated upper control limit and was further substantiated by having six or more consecutive daily accuracy means above the mean line.

Now is a good time to use SPC with Minitab's stage feature to see what the new accuracy performance is. Eventually, the team will recalculate the parameters when SPC shows the new process is stable. Essentially, two SPC Charts are created within one chart. The baseline parameters are used initially in the "Before" titled chart, and then the parameters are recalculated for the period of improvement beginning.

Let's focus on the chart to the right. We see the mean is higher, more favorable, and that is good news. We also see the control limits have changed. What is key now is to judge if the accuracy performance has reached a level of only common cause variation – in other words, is the process stable again? If stable, we have more confidence that accuracy is not only better, but it will remain better. No SPC tests are failing, so we conclude we have succeeded in both improvement and stability.

The team can decide when to use the new parameters without the baseline period. This cycle of charts repeats and should continue to be posted daily until confident performance does not slip. There is no reason to stop posting daily if it is easy to chart and/or the team has improved reliability so well there is no way to fail.

High Reliability Using Statistical Process Control for Daily Scoreboard

After achieving the goal and achieving stability, reliability can be celebrated. How long one should wait before claiming success should consider the timing of variable failure potential. For example, if accuracy was correlated with busy periods, which are seasonal, don't celebrate stability and capability, which is reliability, until at least one busy season has been experienced.

The team and frontline knew the key input variables and achieved high reliability. I have no idea if they have sustained the accuracy rate. I heard they stopped measuring accuracy daily and doubt if they mistake-proofed the variables that earlier had resulted in inaccuracy. Let's hope they keep the SPC going. Again, even the most seasoned sports team wouldn't think of not keeping score during the game.

Figure 5.10 is a representation of their performance while our team was engaged. Again, the data is modified for confidentiality, but the organization achieved and continued to achieve the goal of accuracy being at least the goal.

The SPC daily scorecard and the Capability Analysis are covered next. Capability Analysis is really a reliability analysis, too, when the SPC Chart is included, for the period of potential variable failure.

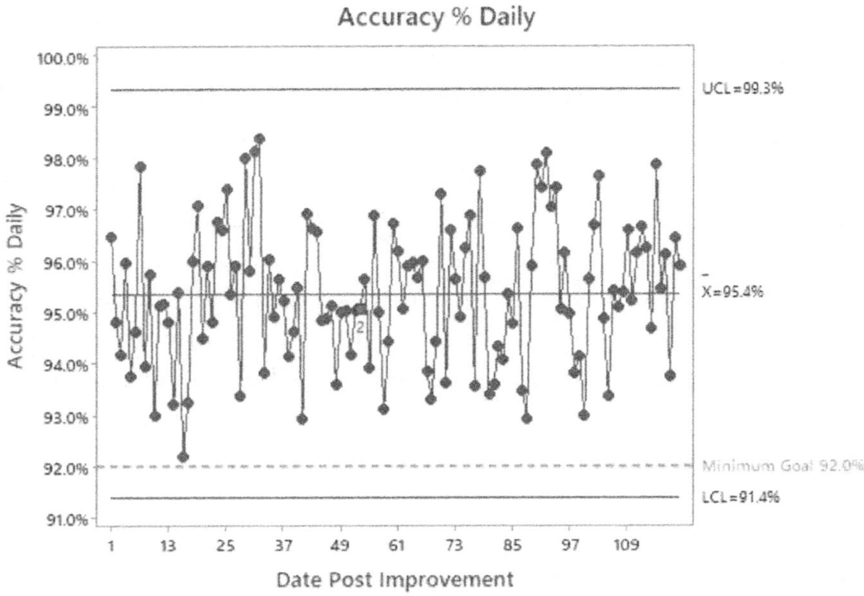

Figure 5.10 Accuracy % daily.

Statistical Process Control Benefit in Measuring Transformations

Statistical process control is my go-to graphic to judge if a transformation has occurred. I would never claim transformative change if SPC did not provide evidence of special cause change. One must be correct in setting baseline periods, using the correct SPC Chart method, and always ensuring the measurement system is capable of measuring reality.

A Capability Analysis goes beyond the graphical view of change and adds information to help teams continuously monitor and improve. SPC is a requirement of a Capability Analysis when the data allows SPC charting. The reason is that capability and reliability have a time component. SPC helps us understand stability – the absence of special cause variation. A Capability Analysis using this story is below.

Capability Analysis

Have you ever seen a Capability Analysis when someone is proclaiming a transformation has occurred? If not, demand one.

If the team working to improve accuracy had a process Capability Analysis before it started problem-solving, the analysis might have resembled the chart in Figure 5.11. Note the 92% goal (LSL is the lower specification limit).

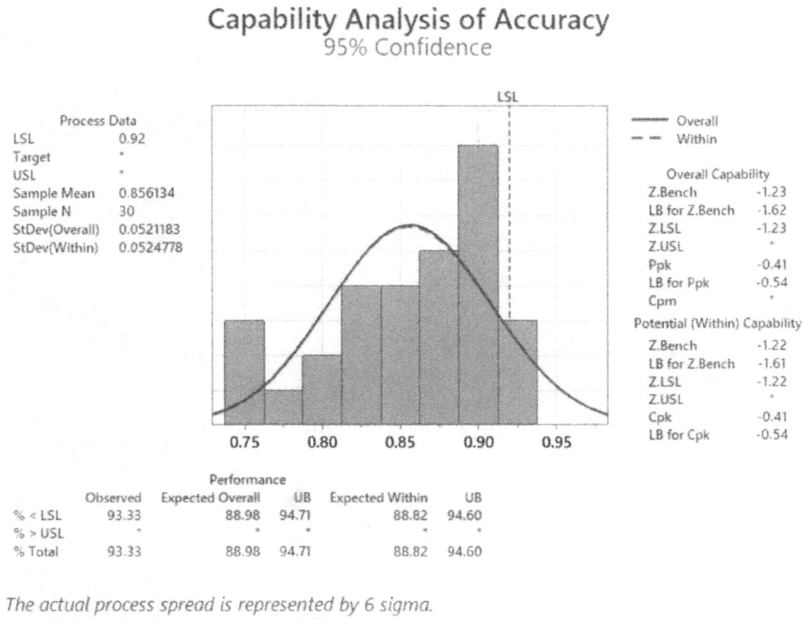

Figure 5.11 Before improvement.

Figure 5.11 shows that the accuracy goal has been reached but is still below goal 93.3% of the days. The “LSL” line is simply the goal of 92% minimum accuracy. Most of the days are to the left of the goal, as we saw in the SPC Chart. But, in the early days of problem-solving, the team working on improvements saw accuracy exceed the goal for the first time. What one does not see in this simple chart is capability over time. There is no confidence in capability if not achieving stability.

Figure 5.12 This is a combination of graphical and statistical analysis making process capability analysis easier. This chart gives us much more information including the test of stability which is required before stating capability.

For the scorecard, the team might want a process Capability Analysis done periodically.

Capability Analysis Including Stability Test Using Statistical Process Control

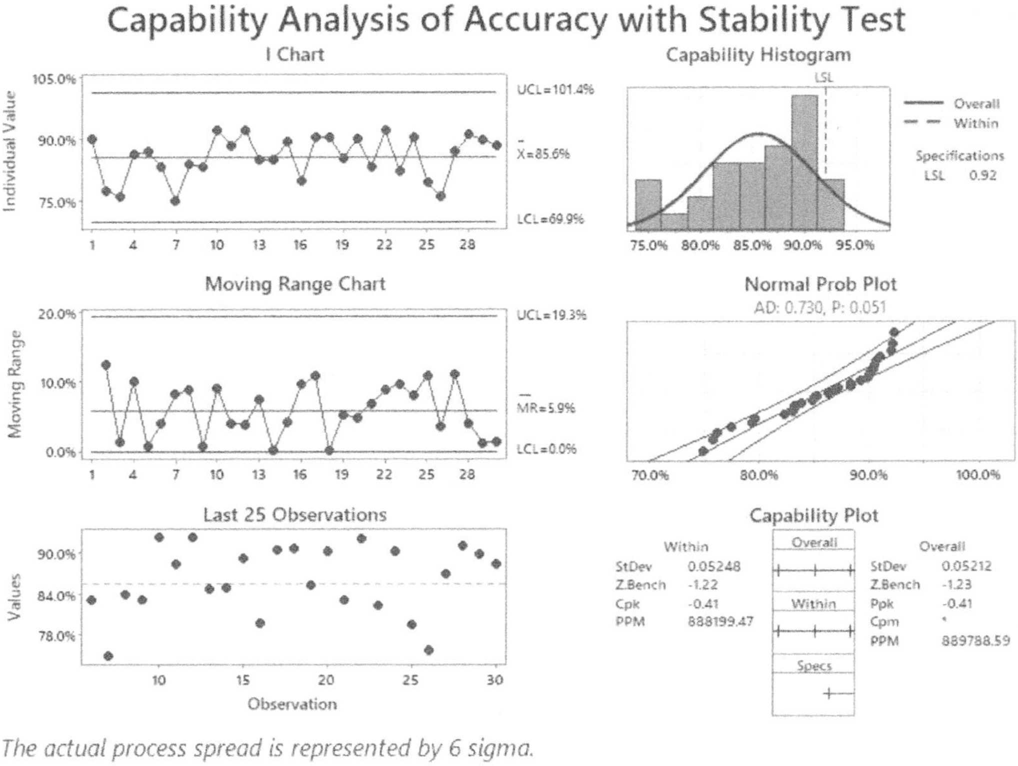

Figure 5.12 Six pack accuracy process capability analysis.

This “Sixpack” of charts from Minitab is helpful in evaluating capability and stability. The top left chart is the familiar SPC Chart. We see no tests failing, so conclude stability is achieved and know we are at a new level of accuracy performance. If the chart showed tests failing, with six or more days below the mean, we could conclude the process is not stable and have no confidence that accuracy is sustaining improvement.

The next Capability Analysis started with data after the team had transformed accuracy. [See Figure 5.13] The chart at the top right shows a histogram of the daily mean %. Note the 92% minimum accuracy goal and that all of the days achieved the goal. The SPC Chart directly to the left shows if stability has sustained. It has, so the team should feel confident that accuracy’s improvement is sustaining and expected to sustain unless something changes in the process. The other charts are used to test assumptions and I cover them in my other books, or one can search for interpreting process capability.

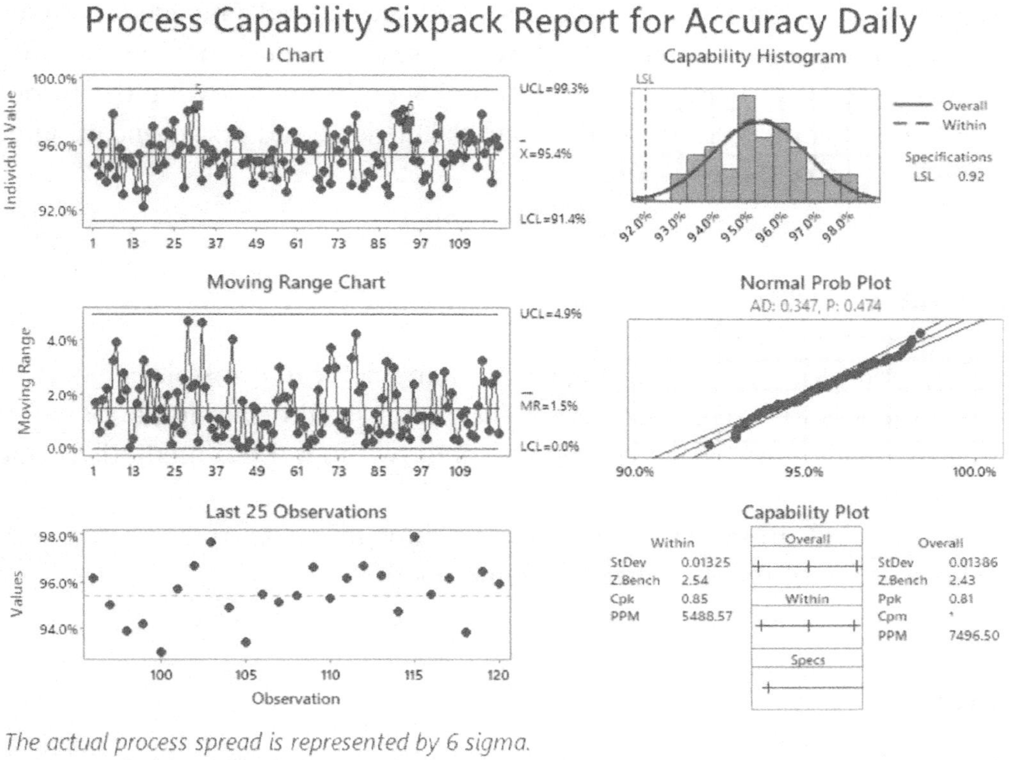

Figure 5.13 Capability in accuracy post-improvement.

We are confident that the process (accuracy) will continue if the process continues as it is. This confidence in stability now allows us to assess the capability in accuracy. First, we may check the bottom left chart to see if the very last days show any instability, and we do not see any pattern, so we conclude even the latest days are stable. Looking at the top right now, we see the same capability chart, but now we have confidence stability has been achieved, and we conclude our new level of capability is achieved.

Capability analyses and SPC should be done based on the data types. I have been assuming normally distributed data after testing for normality prior to the analysis. Using central tendency data, specifically the daily mean, I benefit from the Central Limit Theorem, which states that states the mean of any data will approximate a normal distribution. Thus, this is the reason I use the Individuals SPC Chart method. Refer to my earlier books for more on Capability Analysis and SPC.

I don't expect the transformation to sustain, though, and this is a key lesson for leading to excel and sustain. After sustaining the record-high accuracy and before I closed this consulting event, a new VP to the group heard about these SPC Charts being used. I sensed she did not practice Principle 5: Engage and go see firsthand because she said, "There is no way we are going to force SPC Charts on the frontline." She did not knowing the frontline team and audit were using the charts. This is so sad and demeaning to the intelligence of the workforce.

Summary

The key point for leaders wanting to excel and achieve transformative improvement is to use SPC and Capability Analysis. Proclaiming improvement, especially transformative improvement, without these methods is not to be trusted.

Not using SPC in near-real time is a loss. Imagine a sports team not seeing the score until months after the game ends.

Notes

1. Source: https://www.govinfo.gov/content/pkg/PLAW-107publ204/pdf/PLAW-107publ204.pdf
2. Rother, Mike, and Shook, John, *Learning to See: Value-stream Mapping to Create Value and Eliminate Muda* (Muda is better defined as waste in English), Lean Enterprise Institute, Inc., 1999.
3. Source: https://www.motorolasolutions.com/en_us/about/history/explore-motorola-heritage/cell-phone-development.html

Chapter 6

Transforming Healthcare

Transformations in Safety

Dr. Mark Chassin firmly believed in training to improve quality and safety. He recruited me to help healthcare improve both outcomes, and to help him develop The Joint Commission's Center for Transforming Healthcare. This is one organization named transformation that achieved radical and sustained change. Dr. Chassin practiced all eight principles starting with developing skills in problem-solving. The center working with great healthcare organizations achieved record high safety and quality improvements and more can be read in my prior books, Leading High Reliability Organizations in Healthcare and Utilizing the 3Ms of Process Improvement in Healthcare. The Center for Transforming Healthcare was recognized in the press and our work with solutions scaled out to countless healthcare organizations across the globe. The Center itself does not exist today as Dr. Chassin created but this also highlights that the outcomes are what are important and the leaders and organizations that transformed may fade away. However, Stephanie Mercado, CEO of the National Association for Healthcare Quality (NAHQ), later shares in this chapter a new effort with The Joint Commission. We will stay tuned.

The Center, which I led for Dr. Chassin, was successful in facilitating problem-solving teams with over twenty healthcare organizations to solve four of their most vexing issues. These top healthcare organizations were selected based on their reputation in healthcare quality and having already developed problem-solving using Six Sigma, Lean, and Change Leadership. These organizations identified their most vexing issues and they selected the issues to solve in order of need. Our job at the Center was to facilitate

DOI: 10.4324/9781032639574-6

the collaborations to solve, test, and support rolling out across the globe with those organizations interested. What Dr. Chassin envisioned was not the solutions, but more importantly, the problem-solving process including how each organization can identify its root causes and then specific effective solutions.

Healthcare was full of examples pushing "solutions" that turned out not to work. These ideas consultants or healthcare organizations claimed made improvements have created tremendous waste and frustration because their unsupported idea process oversimplifies the complexity of healthcare processes. Pushing solution ideas without knowing the root causes doesn't work. Worse, the Center's work found root causes can vary across organizations and within an organization's departments. Throwing ideas at unknown causes may exacerbate the problem and is surely a waste of time. Six Sigma, Robust Process Improvement, and my next story of NAHQ with its framework support a methodology of understanding each organization and developing its weaknesses.

Dr. Chassin's Center focused on solving problems and, secondarily, on developing skills where requested, and he was humble to start with TJC's own staff. We picked some of the brightest for the first class, knowing we planned to develop them into problem-solvers with the great acute care organizations participating in the Center. My staff would assist in teaching TJC's staff in Six Sigma, Lean, and how to lead people in change. Mark had hired a consultant to teach a version of Change Management prior to knowing me and that our Six Sigma curricula would cover the need.

We can also learn what happens to transformations when any of the eight principles cease being practiced. The Center's rate of leading collaborations and achieving success in solving major issues decreased from four in the first two years to only a couple in subsequent years. The Center ceased operations after Dr. Chassin's departure. The good news is found in the next story when another organization in the next story independently develops its program for transforming healthcare.

National Association for Healthcare Quality

I have witnessed and been a part of healthcare's attempts to transform healthcare and have always admired one organization in particular because of its dedication to improving healthcare quality, like the Center. Its name is the National Association for Healthcare Quality® (NAHQ).

Its CEO, Stephanie Mercado, granted me an interview to explore her experiences and views on the principles she has applied in transformations. Ms. Mercado is one of the "100 Most Influential People in Healthcare" of 2023 and 2024 by Modern Healthcare.

My purpose of interviewing Stephanie was to capture her leadership experiences in transformations and her work leading NAHQ. While beginning this book, I saw one of Stephanie's promotions of training, and I know readers will value learning from her about her transformations and leadership to excel. This was the second meeting with Stephanie, having earlier spoken with her about volunteering to support the NAHQ mission. I am impressed with NAHQ's mission because it includes helping healthcare solve its most vexing issues with an organization's own talent. This book and volunteering are my way of giving back to help healthcare transform clinical quality, and every transformation I have been a part of was achieved by our own staff and leadership.

Stephanie and I agree that relying solely on consultants to lead problem-solving very seldom achieves much, and NAHQ and The Center for Transforming Healthcare are similar in developing an organization's skills to improve. Following are Stephanie's experiences, and we include and discuss the value of NAHQ's Framework which is also found on NAHQ's website.

She earned her role at the premier healthcare safety organization not by chance after reading her story, vision, and successes.

I think Stephanie's and NAHQ's work in quality improvement training supports my belief in the principle that great leaders train staff in quality and problem-solving throughout the organization.

Stephanie gave me her background, and it is healthcare through and through. Stephanie starts with, "I began working in healthcare in 2002 in the American Orthopedic Association (AOA). I learned what it meant to participate in a nonprofit organization and how medical professionals developed and advanced training curriculums for Graduate Medical Education (GME) students." Stephanie learned graduate pathways in management for physicians while at the AOA, and one of her first grant-funded projects to improve healthcare was to reduce secondary fragility fractures. She worked with Northwestern, NYU, Dartmouth, and other institutions, and they had incredibly positive outcomes. Stephanie was off and running in what would be an illustrious career in healthcare and advancing quality.

In 2007, she was recruited away from AOA to support The American Academy of Physical Medicine and Rehabilitation (AAPM&R). There, she led the development of that profession's first-ever curriculum for practicing

PM&R physicians – asking and answering the question: what does a PM&R physician need to know with years into practice, after GME training is in the rear-view mirror?

In 2013, with her strong experience in workforce curriculum competency development and a keen interest in quality and safety as a lever to advance healthcare, she joined NAHQ.

When she arrived at NAHQ in 2013, Stephanie was surprised to learn that most people working in quality come to it as a second profession. Many began careers in quality after nursing, medicine, engineering, or other roles. She also found little to no educational pathways exist to prepare those working in quality for their roles. She began traveling the country to understand this phenomenon and found that quality structures in healthcare were highly variable – created De novo at each facility, and that the dominant strategy for learning was on-the-job training, led by others who were self-taught. Not only that, but people were saying quality was everyone's job, but no one had defined what that meant.

Stephanie believed there was an untapped space to provide a body of knowledge for quality in healthcare, so she partnered with NAHQ's board, staff, and volunteers to develop the profession's first healthcare competency framework. NAHQ did extensive research to determine the skills necessary to achieve the transformation in quality she and NAHQ believed possible. She and NAHQ developed the NAHQ Quality Competency Framework™ (see Figure 6.1), which details the knowledge and skills to achieve the transformation and categorizes the many skills into eight domains for a higher-level understanding.

This NAHQ Framework would be valued by professionals in healthcare and, today, is recognized nationally and globally as the industry-standard healthcare quality competency Framework. The framework originated from a vision for what was possible in quality and safety and has been the foundation for proving that a coordinated, competent workforce can improve quality and safety outcomes, reduce costs, and improve employee engagement and retention. And today, that vision has been proven out.

Stephanie's experience is that some healthcare organizations have learned and applied Lean, Six Sigma, Safety, and other quality skills, but few have put the entire quality picture together – leveraging a "capital Q" quality mindset. Her vision for NAHQ has positioned NAHQ as the owner of the profession of quality within healthcare and the discipline. Today, NAHQ has successfully leveraged the innovation of NAHQ's Competency Framework and its research to understand where the workforce is and to take them to

Figure 6.1 NAHQ's healthcare quality competency framework.

where they need to be. This reminds me of the consulting cliche, "Meet the client where she is." Listen first to understand current capabilities and then help them develop from that point.

National Association for Healthcare Quality's Healthcare Quality Competency Framework[1]

Plan Your Quality Improvement Journey with the Healthcare Quality Competency Framework

The Framework categorized healthcare quality work into eight domains, comprising

- 29 competency statements
- 486 skill statements

The skills stated in the Framework are

- Required to achieve quality objectives
- Stratified at three distinct levels of progression, from Foundational to Proficient to Advanced
- Not publicly available but are incorporated into the design of NAHQ educational program offerings

Stephanie and NAHQ practiced what they preached by applying the scientific method before announcing their framework. Medicine was an early adopter of the scientific method, applying it to curing patients, and one aspect of the method is to validate hypotheses. We often hear of healthcare borrowing from aviation safety successes, automotive productivity and safety, and electrical power safety, but we all owe Medicine for helping develop the scientific method.

Stephanie and the team believed their framework would help improve quality and thus tested this capability. I wish every consulting firm had the rigor that Stephanie and her team had before proclaiming they have the recipe to transform outcomes.

They set up testing by first creating some standards and then assessing performance against these standards in using the framework. Then they observed the outcomes after applying the framework and were convinced that the Framework resulted in improvement. Once validated, NAHQ began offering its Framework and supporting healthcare organizations in utilizing it. They have been practicing Principle 1: Problem-Solving Skill Development, and the Framework is a result of Principles 3 and 4: SMART radical goals key to achieving the strategic plan that Stephanie led NAHQ in its mission. Building competency in quality is NAHQ's forte and the Framework's value aligns with all the Principles.

Further proof of the value in the NAHQ Quality Competency Framework is found on NAHQ's website. Stephanie's next story is with an organization I have firsthand experience from the Center's work and this is evidence of a transformation in a culture of safety that has continued.

National Association for Healthcare Quality and Lifespan – Leading to Excellence

On the NAHQ website is this story about the NAHQ and Lifespan. *"From the start, quality leaders and the healthcare quality workforce have played a vital role in Lifespan's strategic initiative to deliver operational excellence. The drive for operational excellence has produced major process and performance improvements and saved $12 million in four years for Rhode Island's largest health system, with current projects expected to save another $7.5 million." Lifespan set the strategy first and then organized Cathy and a physician into a centralized Quality organization. The article continues, "In identifying key improvement opportunities, Lifespan's quality leaders and professionals turned their attention to their own function in the organization. That scrutiny initiated "the journey, working closely with the National Association of Healthcare Quality, in totally transforming our quality structures and processes across our organization as well as elevating the competencies of our healthcare quality workforce," said Cathy Duquette, PhD RN NEA-BC CPHQ FNAHQ.*

Lifespan's Cathy Duquette, former Executive Vice President of Quality and Safety and Chief Nursing Officer, and I worked together to improve safety at Lifespan. Lifespan transformed surgical safety, resulting in record high safety levels that sustained for years. She was the Executive Vice President of Nursing Affairs who co-led, with the Executive Vice President of Physician Affairs, system-wide operational excellence efforts.

We see Principle 1: Problem-solving skill development is evident in the website article.

> *Lifespan provided extensive education and training to help its quality workforce master necessary competencies and meet heightened requirements, including training in Six Sigma, TapRoot root-cause analysis, and Failure Modes and Effects Analysis (FMEA), plus certifying as a Lean Green Belt.*

Lifespan applied Principle 6: Manage Risk in its skill development in FMEA. Lifespan was already conversant in FMEA with its success in transforming surgical safety, which began with the FMEA to find the root causes of surgical errors and solve the priority of those highest, most severe risks.

Failure Mode and Effects Analysis is an example of healthcare adopting risk management practices from other industries and making it a standard. Although TJC promoted it in the early 2000s, many organizations preparing for the required survey from TJC applied it only as a "check-the-box" requirement. Lifespan, however, used FMEA as intended by TJC in creating this requirement to identify the many risks to safety and prioritized problem-solving using the FMEA. This story confirms Lifespan sustaining its skills in operational excellence.

Stephanie Mercado on Transformation

In my interview with Stephanie, we discussed the word "transformation" and what it means in healthcare. She believes the word "transformation" is used loosely. She defines it as shifting paradigms. She defines transformation as "A whole new way to look at a problem and create a solution." She continues, "A transformation office is one unit trying to affect everybody. I don't believe transformation is about incremental change. Transformation is an ambitious paradigm shift."

The National Association for Healthcare Quality's perspective is the notion that quality is not a necessary evil or just a regulatory mandate. It (Quality) is the process and the result we are looking to achieve. She mentioned the term Value-Based Care[2] which can mean value in the eyes of the patient and quality of outcomes to a patient is the essence of what the patient wants. Value-Based Care can be confused with the Centers for Medicare and Medicaid's Value-Based Purchasing (VBP) program. The VBP program was designed to reinforce quality, safety, and productivity to provide more value and less waste for patients using Medicare or Medicaid to pay those delivering care. Both Value-Based Care and VBP reinforce quality, and NAHQ's value is two-fold because it can contribute positively to both.

Stephanie suggests organizing all the efforts for quality, including Value-Based Care, within a single workstream or logic model – that encompasses all eight domains of the framework. Quality is not just getting ready for a survey, and it's not just a retrospective chart review. And it's not just Value-Based Care – it is all these things, and more. This perception is what prompted NAHQ to start working toward improvement for capital Q Quality. The core quality and safety are NAHQ-based. She says NAHQ continues innovating to include role-based definitions for quality from the frontline all the way to the board.

Stephanie spoke with Jonathan Perlin, M.D., Ph.D., and President and CEO of TJC, in a recent interview where she raised the perspective that quality as a category should be elevated, and that it means much more than compliance. The NAHQ and TJC have networked and agree that the industry is in urgent need of quality competency and skill development. Having led the startup and first projects for Dr. Chassin's Center for Transforming Healthcare, I see a similar vision of Dr. Chassin and Stephanie at NAHQ – they view their role as getting people ready to do their best work. Stephanie said it well: healthcare has been particularly good at telling people what to do but not good at telling them how to do the work.

Stephanie talked about the process of transformation – not just the results.

A transformation starts with a big vision – a hurdle of something that has never been done before. Principle 3: SMART with Radical Goals is the principle Stephanie is describing. She adds that a leader can articulate the vision and inspire people to be a part of it. Articulating the vision is critical and important with effective communication. The NAHQ's transformational vision was to shift from advancing healthcare one quality professional at a time, and instead to scale competency development and develop new systems and structures for quality management that would ensure results at the bedside.

A big part of achieving radical improvement is being comfortable with being uncomfortable. She adds that we need to help people embrace being uncomfortable. The transformation journey work is critically important. She finds working with boards and governance leadership can be tricky. Stephanie describes the process of making sure people understand where they were, where they are, and where their vision will take them. She talks about all three because it helps to maintain momentum and energy for the cause. As leaders change, especially in board seats, it's important to remind stakeholders how far we have come to build confidence for future success. It's like a teeter-totter, with strategy on one end and operations on the other side of the teeter-totter. Stephanie is describing Principle 7: Celebrate Quick Wins as their journey starts producing results. Celebrating early and frequently builds confidence and motivation.

Transformation Myths

One myth is that a transformation has an endpoint or a deadline. "It is not a transformation if there is no ongoing relevancy," she shares. The NAHQ Framework received wonderful feedback because it outlined the advanced master practitioner skills for those in quality. My staff celebrated and said, "Whew, glad we are done with that." Stephanie coached her staff to hold on. "We did not put in the existing competency skills for a comprehensive framework yet." She made the point that NAHQ was not done yet. "We are just getting started."

We discussed that a transformation should have a time element. When asked, Stephanie answered that decades are a good amount of time for paradigm shifts.

NAHQ sees the value of popular concepts in Quality such as Reliability Engineering, Six Sigma, and other scientific methodologies including Shewhart's and Deming's Plan Do Check Act (PDCA) or PDSA with Study replacing Check. Stephanie shared, at NAHQ, we do not solve problems; we create problem-solvers. Quality tools are incredibly important. We need Force Field Analytics. We need FMEA. The quality toolkit provides value for transformations.

NAHQ finds things may go wrong at the frontline. The NAHQ knows people working on the front lines have been trained differently or not at all in quality and safety. Some do not know about Failure Mode & Effects Analysis, performance improvement, or using data to drive decision-making. NAHQ's mission includes providing support to level up people on the frontline. It offers 1-hour safety training, which is highly effective and follows the story of a surgical case where a wound caused the patient concern and caregivers said all is well.

The National Association for Healthcare Quality coaches frontline staff on how to speak up and escalate their concerns through proper channels. Too often, people are confused about what happens to an issue they identify after a frontline person speaks up. The National Association for Healthcare Quality training supports how to provide feedback that reinforces speaking up and coaches organizations how to carry through on issues to improve. Stephanie reports that NAHQ has outstanding results, and one measure the participants have used to know speaking up is the increase in events recorded. One client of NAHQ reported an 87% participation rate in the client's Press Ganey safety survey. The organization also achieved its first year without a hospital-acquired condition penalty, saving millions of dollars over 3 years.

Stephanie's vision of healthcare's clinical quality starts with NAHQ fundamentally does not believe clinical quality is assessed using the measure of people getting through a survey. The best way to assess is by evidence of high-quality, safe care that is sustainable. "Capital Q Quality" isn't just about clinical quality. It is about the infrastructure required to achieve and sustain quality.

To achieve quality and sustain it, NAHQ focuses on the reduction of variation in the workforce and their competencies. Stephanie often remarks about Dr. Brent James' successes at Intermountain Healthcare in reducing variation. I agree with Stephanie's confidence in Dr. James' teachings. I made a habit of meeting with Dr. Brent James at conferences and always enjoyed his application of Dr. W. Edwards Deming's work and practices to focus on and reduce variation. Stephanie and Dr. James both promote working all day, trying to reduce clinical variability, and NAHQ believes this can be achieved faster and more reliably if we reduce variation in healthcare quality vocabulary, skills, and competencies.

NAHQ's training because of successes like these shared has become the standard for many healthcare organizations in developing problem-solving skills and reducing variation in workforce competencies.

Summary of the National Association for Healthcare Quality Story

Stephanie and NAHQ are achieving and sustaining the mission to improve healthcare clinical quality. We owe it to NAHQ for its work and solutions and its focus on developing skills in healthcare professionals. NAHQ's Quality Competency Framework is the epitome of a principle I find in every transformation. It is Principle 1: Problem-Solving Skill development. It is outcome-based, tested, and validated in improving Quality at Lifespan and many other organizations. The NAHQ's Quality Competency Framework is exactly what is needed to achieve the number one goal of any organization: Improve Outcomes. It is about results, not training hours delivered. The NAHQ team is aware of capability and stability and addresses both as one must to achieve a transformation in reliability. Reliability requires both the capability in meeting performance and sustaining. One without the other is not reliability.

The NAHQ framework is proven to improve capability and capacity for quality and safety, and standardizing the framework itself reduces variation in skill development, which should lead to better and sustained results. Too often I have seen arguments over methodologies, and one that drives waste hypocritically is the debate over Lean vs. Six Sigma. Spending time debating which is better is a sign that the debaters don't know either methodology. National Association for Healthcare Quality avoids the debate altogether, realizing that when Quality is defined as reliably meeting outcomes through time, Drs. Deming, Juran, Crosby, and many others who have transformed quality in many industries found common ground. Lifespan and I applied

Quality Science skills, including FMEA, Capability, and Statistical Process Control, years ago in transforming surgical safety. In addition, Lifespan, with NAHQ took these skills, adding productivity improvement skills, call it Lean if you wish, and transformed to achieve operational excellence measured financially. I look forward to many more successes from NAHQ's work.

Healthcare's Use of Charts in Problem-Solving – Rare Events

Every industry has failures that rarely occur. High Reliability Organizations are defined as having zero or very few failures and if failure occurs, the impact is less than its competitors. Another differentiator of an HRO is found in the use of Principle 2: Utilizing the 3Ms. Many organizations fail to see failure on the horizon because they don't measure rare events, those events that occur very infrequently. HROs measure the process variables that contribute to failure and thus manage to those measures and make it easier to avoid failure. But they may also measure the rare event and this story shares why.

My team was called in to support a healthcare organization working to prevent surgeries on the wrong patient or wrong site/procedure. Fortunately, these occurrences in any one organization are rare, and TJC estimated six occurrences per week across the USA. These are far too many, but few enough that the Individuals type SPC chart is not very effective. A better chart is a rare events chart. Often, the goal is zero. Leaders in this story wanted to achieve zero wrong-site surgeries, and it eventually did. [See Figure 6.2]

Interpretation

Counting the days between these major egregious failures allows a team to validate when improvement is occurring. The chart above is representative of a hospital organization that had five wrong patient or wrong-site surgeries (WSS) in a couple of years. The goal was simple - eliminate all these failures.

The daily scorecard is always our go-to chart when failure is possible daily. WSS failure is much less likely on a daily basis, so we added a chart for these outcomes when the wrong patient was found in the surgical process or the wrong site was operated on.

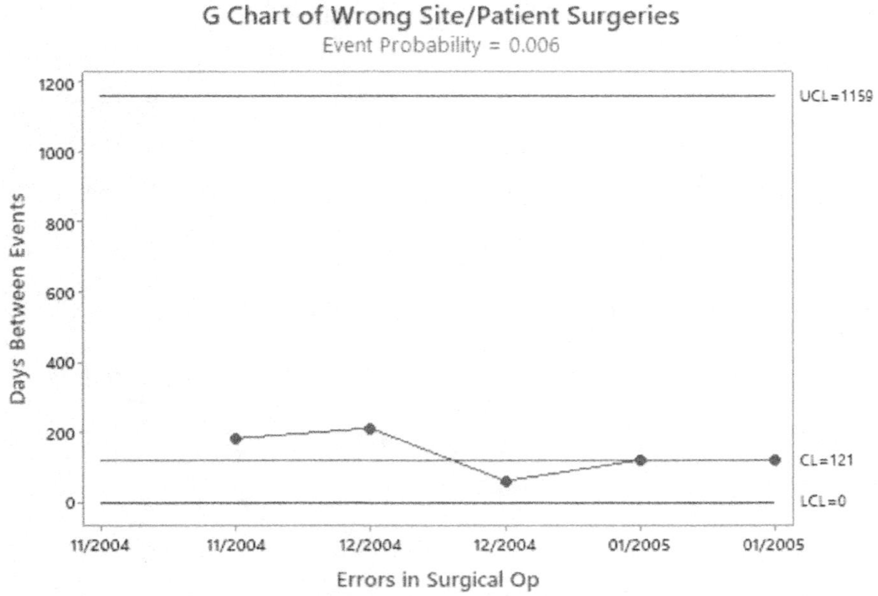

Figure 6.2 G Chart.

We will always use the daily chart as well, but the daily chart will be tracking the variables that may result in a poor outcome. Think of this strategy as focusing on input variables daily and keeping score on the outcomes less frequently. This allows powerful correlation analysis, which can identify the input variables that contribute to the poor outcome in a root-cause analysis, and then this same chart will give us earlier verification if better outcomes are occurring. Lower the slips, lapses, and mistakes that cause the wrong patient to be wheeled in or the wrong site to be operated on.

Below is the chart of these input variables. The surgical team started plotting and displaying these charts in the areas of the hospital where the slips, lapses, or mistakes occur. [See Figure 6.3]

Once the team identified the variables causing the WSS events, they plotted the occurrences of these variables and continued to problem-solve.

The team eliminated 100% of the wrong patient and wrong-site surgical failures for years until I no longer heard from the leadership. The Peri-Op Nurse leader took a position at another large healthcare organization in another state and remained successful.

The SPC chart of outcomes was maintained for a time, and the team felt that keeping score of the slips, lapses, and mistakes was the best "game to play" to eliminate the WSS events. It proved successful for years. If I heard of another WSS event, the first question would be to see the daily chart. I would not be surprised if they told me they quit plotting long ago.

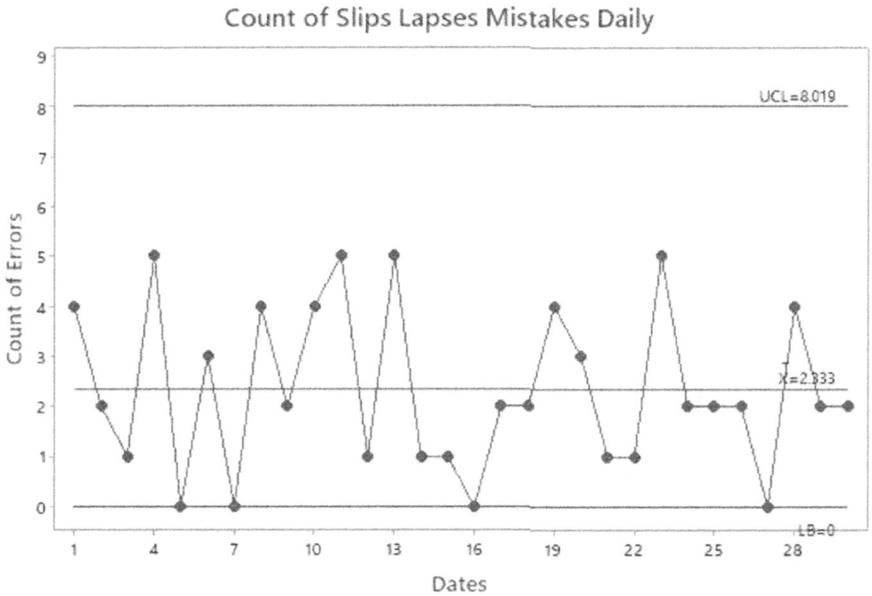

Figure 6.3 Slips lapses mistakes.

Leading to excel and achieving high reliability are accomplished using statistical methods. It is much easier, and the only thing that stands in the way of not utilizing these statistical measures is a lack of knowledge in these methods. Knowing them and not using them is not leading to excel. There

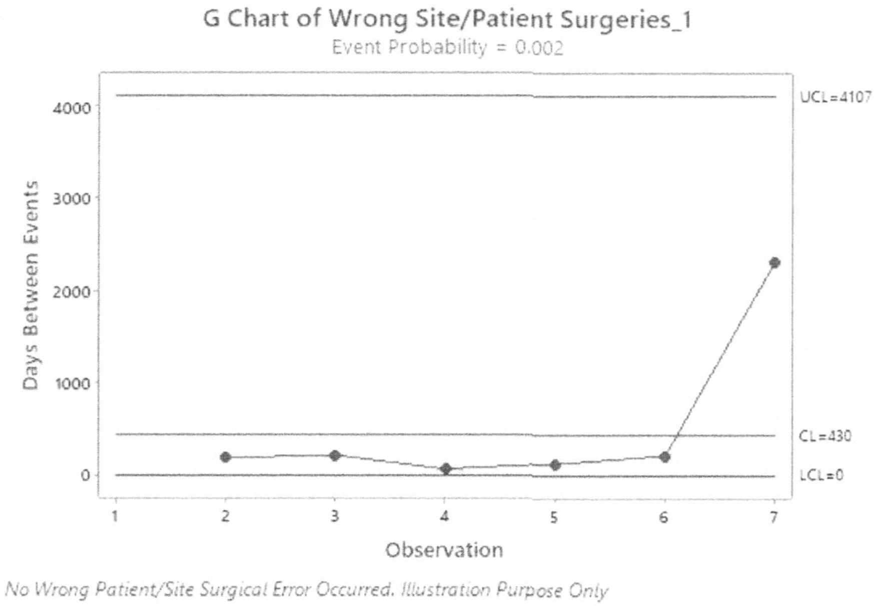

Figure 6.4 G Chart.

are people trained in these methods in every industry I have worked in and this book, along with my earlier books, should equip every organization to learn and apply them successfully. And plenty more books on the subject and classes exist.

The G Chart of actual WSS failures (see Figure 6.4) was never plotted because the team never experienced another event for years. I share the value of the chart to illustrate how this SPC G Chart shows progress. The number of days between events will increase as teams improve.

Summary

Healthcare joins the aviation, nuclear power, and USA Department of Defense industries in striving to become High Reliability Organizations. Healthcare is fragmented and is unlike the auto industry after World War II, when essentially three manufacturers dominated the auto industry. The Big Three cooperated and supported the entire supply chain in improving quality. Healthcare organizations like the NAHQ overcome this fragmentation by providing skills that support and share the principles. The NAHQ's Quality Competency Framework spans healthcare organizations. The Joint Commission's Center for Transforming Healthcare pioneered spreading the quality science across healthcare using Lean Six Sigma collaborations and NAHQ is filling a gap since the Center was closed. In November 2024, Stephanie Mercado announced a joint venture with TJC to improve quality sharing. If all eight principles are taught and applied, their work together has potential.

There are exciting transformations in healthcare regarding patient safety. The utilization of these principles is evident in every transformation covered in chapters on healthcare. Leaders applying the eight principles validate these principles. Missing any of the principles and seeing the resulting marginal or short-term results further verifies the need for all eight, such as in Principle 8: Keep utilizing the 3Ms. We have seen that whenever a leader stops promoting measurement frequently and before a process is capable of sustaining, outcomes fade.

Notes

1. Available at https://nahq.org/nahq-intelligence/competency-framework/
2. Source: https://www.cms.gov/priorities/innovation/key-concepts/value-based-care.

Chapter 7

Leading to Excel

Leading anything to excel beyond your competitors' level of performance outcomes is a daunting task but one filled with fun, hardship, cultural discoveries, and friends won and lost. Looking back at the stories shared in this book, not one story goes without a leadership element. This does not mean the leader was an executive; in fact, none of these transformations were accomplished with an executive in the day-to-day role leading change. It is not a principle that an executive must lead a transformation. Examples of executives achieving transformations are all around, including Elon Musk in his SpaceX program which is transforming space travel. Henry Ford transformed the auto industry manufacturing with his flow assembly but more importantly, he helped create the middle class with higher pay for so many. Steve Jobs at Apple led the shift in cellular phone technology with the iPhone.

The Eaton transformations were built on a crisis shared by an executive, but the vision came from non-executives. Executives supported those transforming outcomes because many require a shift in strategy, financial resources, and sometimes breaking down barriers from people who are resisting. The transformations at Eaton were all led by mid-level managers. Some of the leaders became executives, so maybe that points to personal gains from transforming performance. I am confident the transformations we achieved have helped me progress throughout my career, but regardless, for every fortunate person who was promoted, there are a hundred who elected to enjoy whatever level in the organization they are and have lasting great memories of the transformation period.

Transforming an organization does not guarantee transforming performance. Again, structure follows strategy. Don't reorganize until the strategy

DOI: 10.4324/9781032639574-7

requires it, if at all. It is all too common to create a transformation office and then see no transformative outcomes.

Promotions should occur after transformations. I can name folks who were promoted to achieve a transformation yet who achieved little. This is not to blame the individual because often there was no strategy, no KPI to radically improve, little budget and resources to train people in problem-solving, and worse, no utilization of the 3Ms before the transformation and after the effort. So, the organization misses key learning, probably demoted the person, and thus will probably repeat again with another poor soul in the organization's thinking of creating a transformation organization instead of applying the eight principles.

If prior efforts have not succeeded and the organization is desperate to achieve excellence and perhaps even cease to exist, begin not with organizing a group to transform but by leading with Principle 1: Develop problem-solving skills. At Eaton, we were taught problem-solving first, and everyone was included from the frontline through middle management. We continued to deploy those skills and techniques throughout the transformation journey. Problem-solving skills can occur after other principles, especially Principle 4: Strategy and then knowing what skills will support the strategy. Lincoln capitalized on having problem-solving skills that opened our eyes to the fact that we needed to refine our strategy to compete.

I think this is why organizing a transformation office has seldom resulted in transformative outcomes in organizations where I worked or consulted. Saying you want something is easy. Achieving excellence is hard and takes every skill, technically, culturally, and emotionally, one can muster. Maybe if one must create a transformation office, ensure the executive leading it has achieved excellence, is well-versed in all eight Principles, and uses these eight Principles in recruiting the transformation team.

Like any good HR hiring process, bias the interviewing toward asking behavioral questions vs. "What would you do" questions. Use problem-solving and Principle 2: The 3Ms to structure your questions. I learned in promoting folks that promotions are best based on achievements that occurred – not based on promises or expectations of those achievements. I could tell stories of times I promoted first, expecting outcomes to change, which never came. In fact, I learned with our band's road crew when I was in my early 20s. They kept asking for higher pay and they were good at what they did. So, we raised their pay with their agreement they would become better tech support and do more of the setup we musicians did. Alas, we musicians never got from them what we wanted. At one company early in my corporate career, I promoted a person who did very well at his job only to see him fail in the role I promoted him to. This was not fair to him or the organization, and I take responsibility. Promoting or organizing to achieve transformative change should be rethought. Lead with a strategy and the eight principles soon thereafter.

Absolutely focus as a leader on Principle 5: Engage and Go See. The Eaton manufacturing process transformation had a catalyst. Earlier I discussed when Wayne had interviewed a candidate who mentioned the Harley Davidson Plant near Milwaukee, WI, for its Just-In-Time transformation. Wayne, Al, and I drove the four hours to meet with Harley's team and came away with the ideas that we could do it and the motivation to improve our facility. Zero Defects learned at SKF became the cause and motivation to achieve zero surgical errors in healthcare. Seeing is believing is true. We talk about cultural resistance, and instead of trying to talk an organization into transforming performance practices, Principle 5: Engage and Go See by empowering others to go and see for themselves. Don McCann knew Wayne's, Al's, and my ideas would be better received by offering the Union President and sidekick a chance to go see the Harley plant, and they did. They came back fully supporting the transformation efforts.

Principle 5 Includes Go Experience Firsthand Via Reading

Another great practice of Principle 5 is to "Go" via reading. Read books about transformations and leaders who excel. I give Tom Peters credit for much of my learning in leading organizations. His book, *In Search of Excellence*[1], shared stories of companies who had achieved excellence and competitive advantage, including the Department of Defense, Sewell Cadillac, and more. He tells the story of flying sorties improved after engaging with the pilots and flight maintenance crews and discovering root causes, including having parts to keep planes operating. Sewell Cadillac exists today, at least by name, and Tom talked about its leader's empathy and empowerment of his teams.

Some of our transformations were improved with after reading stories shared in the Harvard Business Review. I read every publication from the start of my Executive MBA in the late 1980s through my time leading healthcare in the early 2010s.

Books that are not business-related include the Bible, books on the history of transformative times especially from the evolution of Homo Sapiens, the Renaissance, and innovation. I try to pull something from anything I read and put it to use.

Music is an interesting transformation story. There have been transformations in music, yet at the same time, my cover band is probably most popular for not transforming the music we cover. We receive many compliments for reproducing the music as the original artist performed it. I guess we can see that transforming could be competitively a no – for a cover band, especially a Tribute band. A tribute band's success and popularity is to reproduce the music as much as possible of the band that they are trying to reproduce musically. Some tribute bands even dress and act like the original artists. So, this is a lesson that not everything needs to be transformed to achieve a strategy.

Would one consider what became Classical music a transformation from some other type of music? I think so because, no one had ever composed works like Beethoven, Mozart, and Strauss composed. Their works became the music of the day. In my lifetime, we heard rock and roll for the first time, although much has been written about how it transformed from Blues, Gospel, and Classical among other genres. I find it interesting when this genre was named Classical. I don't think Beethoven called his music Classical at the time he composed.

Root Cause Analysis of Failing to Excel

As you probably expect, I see failing to practice all eight Principles as the root cause of failing to transform outcomes. It is not to blame a leader because we have already proved one does not need the title to lead anything to excel. Out of the eight Principles, I see not utilizing the 3Ms as a common cause of failed improvements in outcome. Healthcare's Value-Based Purchasing[2] is an example. I found The Centers for Medicare and Medicaid's idea to monetarily reward and punish for the quality of healthcare promising because that is business 101. But it has proven to be underwhelming in improving health outcomes. Value-Based Purchasing was to be complementary to Value-Based Care by monetarily reinforcing acute care healthcare organizations to improve outcomes or punish those organizations with lower reimbursement for trailing behind their competition.

Whenever I was called in to help healthcare organizations, we immediately practiced Principles 2 and 4 by measuring how they performed relative to their competitors across many measures used by the Centers for Medicare and Medicaid Services (CMS) to score firms. We had already highlighted a strategy to maximize financial outcomes. Utilizing the 3Ms for them, I shared the measures CMS had of their performance, I made it easier for the healthcare organization to prioritize what to improve first, and then my consulting was measured by helping them manage to the measures – to get better. I even developed a Value-Based Purchasing calculator that used publicly available data from CMS to calculate the financial impact by measure and in total. The organization where I was Vice President called for this analysis on hundreds of acute care organizations, and we were contracted in some to help them problem-solve based on optimizing the financial outcomes.

My consulting strategy is to teach them how to fish, the saying goes. Instead of swarming in, piling in my consulting staff, and solving problems for them, I preferred to show and coach the organization's own skilled problem-solvers. An example close to my home is an acute care organization raised its patient experience scores to record highs while another large medical center improved patient safety in the targeted areas.

Too often missing were the organization's problem-solving skills, Principle 1, and Principle 3: SMART radical goals. Very seldom was the organization striving for anything that would require a transformation. Exceptions existed, including the University of Pennsylvania Medical Center, which strove for Zero Preventable Mortality and another large healthcare organization's goal for Zero Wrong Site Surgeries. They made many major improvements, having contracted with us to develop Six Sigma and Lean skills and coach multidisciplinary teams in their safety-focused projects. Penn Medicine, as of 2024 is still teaching versions of the course and continues to empower clinical caregivers as well as administrative employees with this training and project support. I leave it to Penn Medicine to judge if transformational.

Summary

I have covered all eight principles and would love to hear from you in your journey to excel. Contact me at rpmexecauthor@gmail.com. I have been very fortunate to have these experiences, and my wish is that this book gives a little back and you achieve transforming your organization's outcomes. Let me know as you go.

Notes

1. Peters, Thomas J., and Waterman, Robert H., 1982, *In Search of Excellence*,. Warner Books, NY, 1982.
2. Found at: https://www.cms.gov/priorities/innovation/key-concepts/value-based-care

Index

Made in the USA
Monee, IL
13 September 2026

62980172R00109